MENSA® PRESENTS:
THE BIG BOOK OF
BRAIN BENDERS

200 PUZZLES AND RIDDLES
FROM THE SMARTEST BRAND
IN THE WORLD

DAVID MILLAR

Skyhorse Publishing

Copyright © 2018, 2021, 2023 by David Millar

Content from this book has been previously published in *Mensa® Brain Games* (ISBN: 978-1-5107-3862-1) and *Mensa® Ultimate Brain Benders* (ISBN: 978-1-5107-5884-1)

Skyhorse Publishing books may be purchased in bulk at special discounts for sales promotion, corporate gifts, fund-raising, or educational purposes. Special editions can also be created to specifications. For details, contact the Special Sales Department, Skyhorse Publishing, 307 West 36th Street, 11th Floor, New York, NY 10018 or info@skyhorsepublishing.com.

Skyhorse® and Skyhorse Publishing® are registered trademarks of Skyhorse Publishing, Inc.®, a Delaware corporation.

Visit our website at www.skyhorsepublishing.com.

10 9 8 7 6 5 4 3 2 1

Library of Congress Cataloging-in-Publication Data is available on file.

Cover design by Kai Texel

ISBN: 978-1-5107-7859-7

Printed in China

CONTENTS

Puzzles 1

Answer Keys 207

    Arrow Maze 208

    Black Holes 210

    Chess Sudoku 212

    Cube Logic 212

    In Memoriam 213

    Maze 214

    Numcross 215

    Pent Words 217

    Rearrangement 217

    Ringed Planet 218

    Rows Garden 219

    Story Logic 220

    Symbol Sums 222

    Tetra Grid 224

    UFO Sighting 227

    Word Sudoku 227

Exercise Your Mind at American Mensa 228

PUZZLES

Cube Logic 1

Which of the four foldable patterns can be folded
to make the cube displayed?

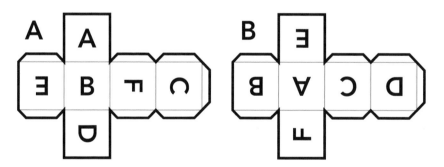

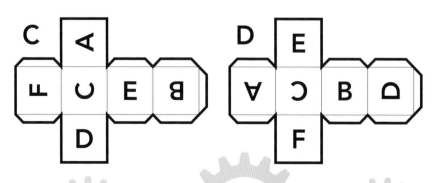

Numcross 1

Use the provided clues to fill the grid with numbers. No entry may start with a 0.

A	B	C		D	E
F				G	
		H	I		
J	K				
L			M	N	O
P			Q		

Across

A. C down - H across
D. A perfect cube
F. Digits that sum to 10
G. P across - 10
H. B down converted to binary from base 10
J. Consecutive digits in descending order
L. The B-___s
M. Blink ____
P. ____ Cent
Q. Another perfect cube

Down

A. Largest answer that satisfies I down
B. A down - 2
C. Digits that sum to 6
D. K down × 2
E. Digits that sum to 5
I. A down converted to binary from base 10
J. B down × 35
K. 8 × G across
N. Every even digit is used in this entry or D down
O. A perfect square

Arrow Maze 1

Each move, jump from your current square to another square in the same row, column, or diagonal as permitted by the arrow or arrows provided. There are no dead ends here. Can you get from Start to Finish in 10 steps?

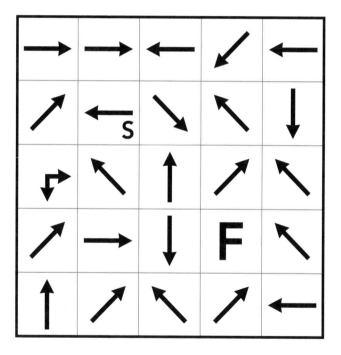

Tetra Grid 1

Drop each of the shapes into the grid in the order provided to spell ten six-letter words. Clues for the words have been provided next to the grid.

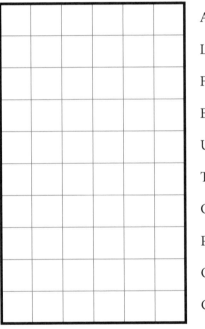

A vegan milk source

Leave

Flavor

Earlyish meal

Unit of time

Two, eleven, or eighty, e.g.

Gift wrap component

Photography tool

Original copy

Celiac sufferer's bane

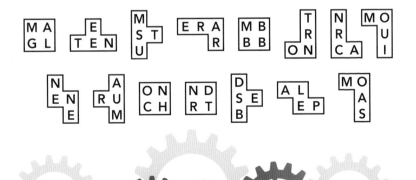

Word Sudoku 1

In the sudoku grid, enter one of each of six unique letters into each row, column, and boldly-outlined six-celled rectangle without repetition.

			S		
		N			P
P				O	
H	O	T			
		O		H	
		N	S		

PHOTONS

Maze 1

In this maze, you may cross under paths using tunnels where indicated by arrows.

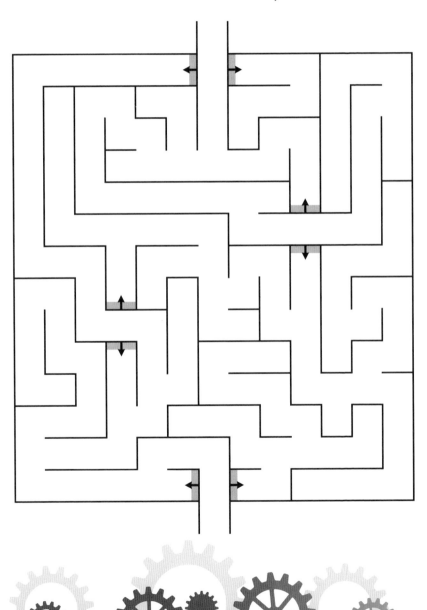

Pent Words 1

Split the grid into shapes, and use the clues
provided to spell five-letter words across each row
and within each shape. Shape clues include an
outline, but the shape may be rotated or reflected.

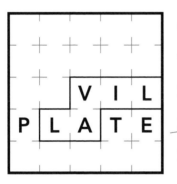

Create

Tall structure

Heavy cartoon prop

Diner necessity

Do away with

 Royal headwear

 Slim down

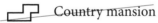 Country mansion

 Following

Make fun

Two words have been completed to get you started!

Story Logic 1

Four vehicles are in the shop for a wash and detail, and the work orders got mixed up. Use the clues provided to match the vehicle to the owner's scheduled pickup time, and the wash package and air freshener scent picked by the owner.

		Wash Package				Pickup Time				Air Freshener			
		Level 1: Express	Level 2: Basic	Level 3: Plus	Level 4: Supreme	3:30 PM	4:00 PM	4:30 PM	5:00 PM	Berried Treasure	Brisk Lake	Hot Breeze	Tropical Wood
Vehicle	Ford												
	Honda												
	Jeep												
	Toyota												
Air Freshener	Berried Treasure												
	Brisk Lake												
	Hot Breeze												
	Tropical Wood												
Pickup Time	3:30 PM												
	4:00 PM												
	4:30 PM												
	5:00 PM												

The Honda's pickup time is immediately between the pickup times for the Ford and the Jeep, in some order.

The vehicle getting the Hot Breeze air freshener is being picked up immedately after the vehicle getting the Express wash package.

The vehicle getting the Plus wash package is not the recipient of the Tropical Wood air freshener.

The Toyota's wash package is either the Plus package or the Supreme package.

The owner who picked the Supreme wash package also picked the Berried Treasure air freshener.

The Toyota is scheduled to be picked up immediately before the vehicle whose owner wants the Brisk Lake air freshener.

The Ford's pickup time is exactly one hour after the pickup time for the vehicle getting the Express package.

Symbol Sums 1

The sums of five combinations of symbols have been provided. What is the value of each individual symbol?

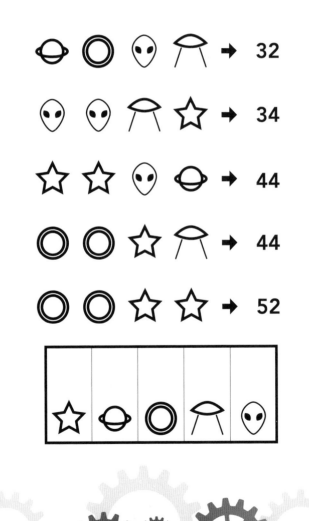

Numcross 2

Use the provided clues to fill the grid with numbers. No entry may start with a 0.

A	B	■	C	D	E
F		■	G		
H		I		■	■
■		J		K	L
M	N		■	O	
P			■	Q	

Across

A. N down × 2
C. P across - 5
F. 5 × O across
G. C across + K down
H. K down × 3
J. Consecutive digits in descending order
M. A perfect square
O. M down - 1
P. Another perfect square
Q. (3 × N down) + 1

Down

A. A multiple of M down
B. Digits that sum to 10
C. 5 × L down
D. N down + 10
E. 2 × A Across
I. B down × 7
K. C across × 3
L. A palindrome
M. The square root of M across
N. D down - 10

Tetra Grid 2

Drop each of the shapes into the grid in the order provided to spell ten six-letter words. Clues for the words have been provided next to the grid.

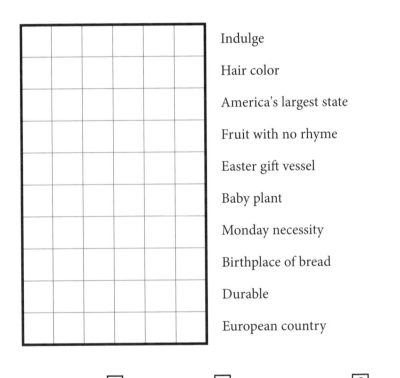

Indulge

Hair color

America's largest state

Fruit with no rhyme

Easter gift vessel

Baby plant

Monday necessity

Birthplace of bread

Durable

European country

UFO Sighting 1

Use the clues provided to find five answers
containing the letters UFO.

F _ O U _   Essential for baking

_ O F U _ _ _   Vegetarian Thanksgiving dish

F O U _ _ _ _   Creator

O U _ F _ _   Clothing

F O _ _ U _ _   Possible cookie insert

Arrow Maze 2

Each move, jump from your current square to another square in the same row, column, or diagonal as permitted by the arrow or arrows provided. There are no dead ends here. Can you get from Start to Finish in 10 steps?

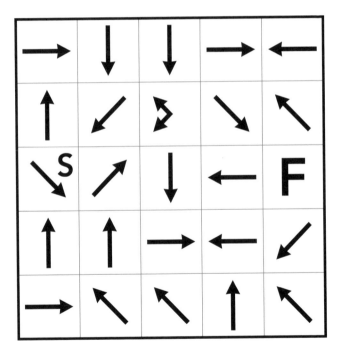

Cube Logic 2

Which of the four foldable patterns can be folded
to make the cube displayed?

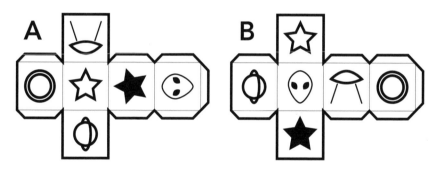

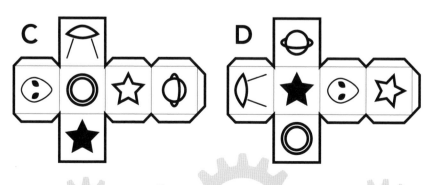

Maze 2

In this maze, you may cross under paths using tunnels where indicated by arrows.

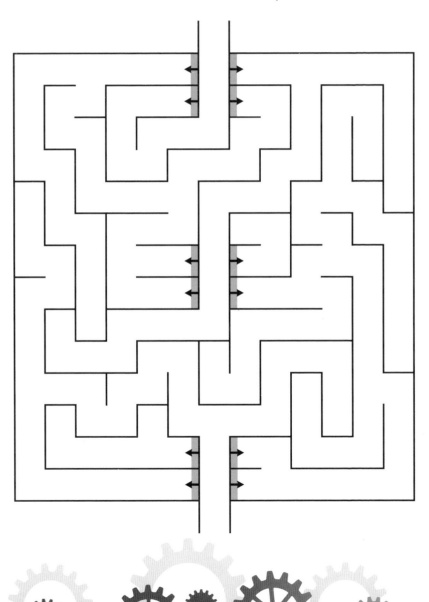

Pent Words 2

Split the grid into shapes, and use the clues provided to spell five-letter words across each row and within each shape. Shape clues include an outline, but the shape may be rotated or reflected.

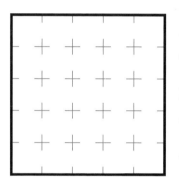

Artist medium

Take

Barber shop

Water barrier

Golf tournaments

 Against all odds

Carb-laden dish

Solo

Chip maker

Ski locale

Word Sudoku 2

In the sudoku grid, enter one of each of six unique letters into each row, column, and boldly-outlined six-celled rectangle without repetition.

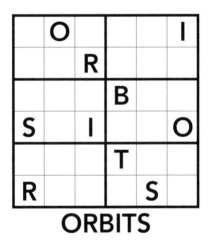

ORBITS

Rearrangement 1–2

Rearrange the letters in the phrase "FANCY GIRL SUE" to spell something Sue might see in the sky.

Rearrange the letters in the phrase "OAT CRACKER" to spell a dessert that sounds much better than an oat cracker.

Numcross 3

Use the provided clues to fill the grid with numbers. No entry may start with a 0.

	A	B		
C			D	
E			F	G
H			I	
	J	K		
		L		

Across

A. A perfect square
C. (L across × 30) + 3
E. F across squared
F. Another perfect square
H. Another perfect square
I. K down × 8
J. C across - 43
L. F across × 3

Down

A. A perfect cube
B. E down + 1
C. J across + 82
D. Consecutive digits in descending order
E. Another perfect cube
G. B down in reverse
I. I across - 1
K. Another perfect cube

Symbol Sums 2

The sums of five combinations of symbols have
been provided. What is the value of each
individual symbol?

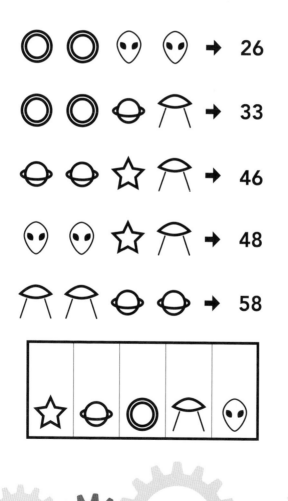

Rearrangement 3–4

Rearrange the letters in the phrase "WHY A FIFTH CIGAR" to spell something that might last a very long time.

Rearrange the letters in the phrase "ONLY A LEOTARD" to spell a windy place where protective clothing may be needed.

Arrow Maze 3

Each move, jump from your current square to another square in the same row, column, or diagonal as permitted by the arrow or arrows provided. There are no dead ends here. Can you get from Start to Finish in 10 steps?

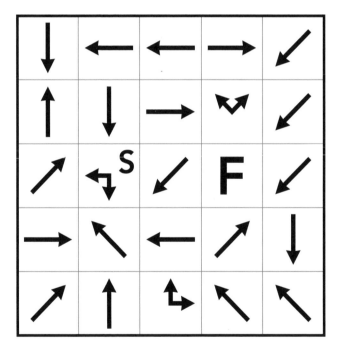

Tetra Grid 3

Drop each of the shapes into the grid in the order provided to spell ten six-letter words. Clues for the words have been provided next to the grid.

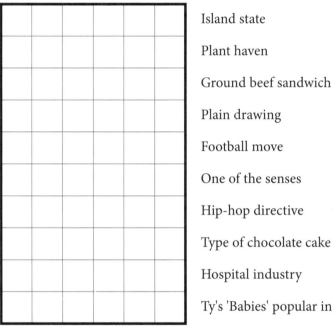

Island state

Plant haven

Ground beef sandwich

Plain drawing

Football move

One of the senses

Hip-hop directive

Type of chocolate cake

Hospital industry

Ty's 'Babies' popular in 90's

Pent Words 3

Split the grid into shapes, and use the clues provided to spell five-letter words across each row and within each shape. Shape clues include an outline, but the shape may be rotated or reflected.

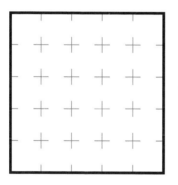

Mix

Friend in Argentina

Under

Intensity

Sense

 Correct

Snow structure

Attribute

Jails

Bestow

Story Logic 2

Going vegetarian is difficult for hardcore burger lovers. Use the judging notes from this veggie burger cookoff to match the cook with their burger's protein, flavor profile, and rank.

		Rank				Burger				Protein			
		First Place	Second Place	Third Place	Fourth Place	Au Jus-Style	Southwest	Teriyaki	Tikka Masala	Black Beans	Lentils	Mushrooms	Tempeh
Cook	Rakesh												
	Sal												
	Tanya												
	Victor												
Protein	Black Beans												
	Lentils												
	Mushrooms												
	Tempeh												
Burger	Au Jus-Style												
	Southwest												
	Teriyaki												
	Tikka Masala												

The burger made from tempeh was better than the burger made by Sal.

The Southwest burger was better than the one with the lentil patty.

The Tikka Masala burger was not a black bean burger.

The black bean burger took 2nd place in the cookoff.

The Teriyaki burger ranked just one level higher than the Au Jus-Style burger.

Tanya's tikka masala burger was beat by both the Teriyaki and the tempeh burger.

Either Rakesh or Victor made the mushroom burger.

Victor's Southwest burger beat Rakesh's burger.

Cube Logic 3

Which of the four foldable patterns can be folded
to make the cube displayed?

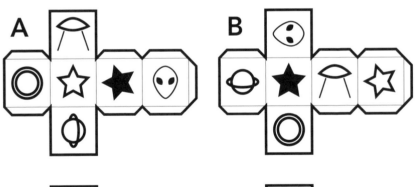

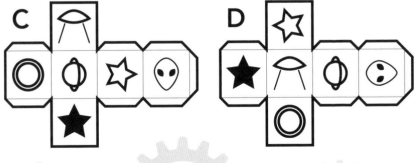

Word Sudoku 3

In the sudoku grid, enter one of each of six unique letters into each row, column, and boldly-outlined six-celled shape without repetition.

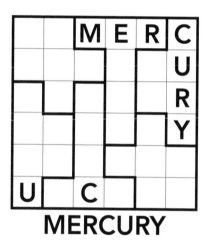

MERCURY

Numcross 4

Use the provided clues to fill the grid with numbers. No entry may start with a 0.

Across

A. Days since you took your love away (Sinéad)
C. O down - 2
E. P across × O down
G. N down + 1
H. Year of the debut of the first Harry Potter book
J. Consecutive digits in ascending order
L. 1 + half of N down
M. C across × L across
P. O down + 2
Q. A perfect square

Down

A. Days since you took your love away (Prince)
B. N down - 5
C. An anagram of F down
D. A palindrome
F. I down - B down
I. A across × G across
J. Consecutive digits in descending order
K. M across - 30
N. A perfect cube
O. The name of Adele's debut album

Arrow Maze 4

Each move, jump from your current square to another square in the same row, column, or diagonal as permitted by the arrow or arrows provided. There are no dead ends here. Can you get from Start to Finish in 8 steps?

Tetra Grid 4

Drop each of the shapes into the grid in the order provided to spell ten six-letter words. Clues for the words have been provided next to the grid.

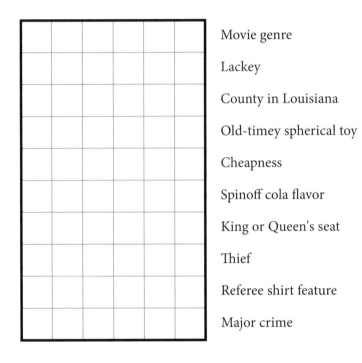

Movie genre

Lackey

County in Louisiana

Old-timey spherical toy

Cheapness

Spinoff cola flavor

King or Queen's seat

Thief

Referee shirt feature

Major crime

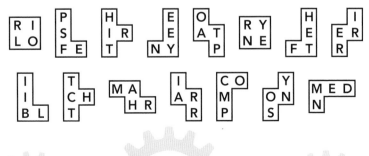

Symbol Sums 3

The sums of five combinations of symbols have been provided. What is the value of each individual symbol?

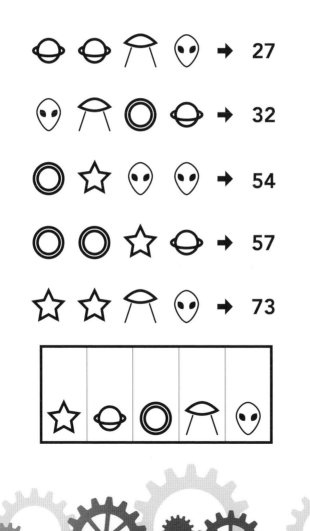

Story Logic 3

It's a popular day for appliance deliveries. Use the clues provided to match the customer with the street upon which they live, appliance they're having installed, and which container has it.

		Street				Container #				Appliance			
		Mulberry St.	Ninth St.	Owosso St.	Palm Ridge Way	AB456	CC179	CC341	DM446	Dryer	Refrigerator	Stove	Washer
Customer	Ms. Campbell												
	Mr. Daivari												
	Mr. Evans												
	Mrs. Fredrickson												
Appliance	Dryer												
	Refrigerator												
	Stove												
	Washer												
Container #	AB456												
	CC179												
	CC341												
	DM446												

The stove, which is being delivered to Mulberry St., is not for Mr. Evans.

The refrigerator is in container number DM446.

Container number AB456 is going to either Owosso St. or Palm Ridge Way.

Mulberry St. and Palm Ridge Way are the two destinations of the containers with numbers starting in CC.

The container containing the washer is one of the two with the number starting in CC.

Ms. Campbell lives in a house on Ninth St.

Mr. Daivari's appliance is in one of two containers: either AB456 or DM446.

Mrs. Fredrickson is the recipient of the appliance in container number CC179.

Maze 3

In this maze, you may cross under paths using tunnels where indicated by arrows.

Word Sudoku 4

In the sudoku grid, enter one of each of six unique letters into each row, column, and boldly-outlined six-celled shape without repetition.

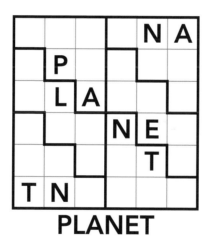

PLANET

Rearrangement 5–6

Rearrange the letters in the phrase "A CACAO WHICH FIGS PITY" to spell a scenic route upon which you might take a road trip and eat cacao.

Rearrange the letters in the phrase "CHICHI SEES RELIEF" to spell a food that a hungry person like ChiChi would love to eat.

Symbol Sums 4

The sums of five combinations of symbols have been provided. What is the value of each individual symbol?

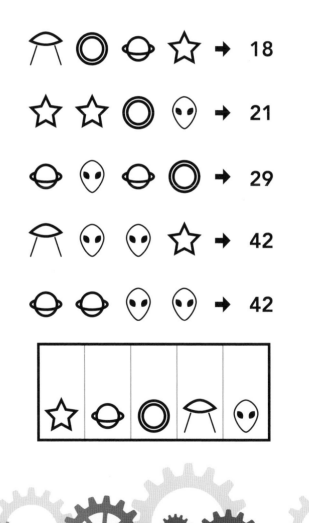

Arrow Maze 5

Each move, jump from your current square to another square in the same row, column, or diagonal as permitted by the arrow or arrows provided. There are no dead ends here. Can you get from Start to Finish in 8 steps?

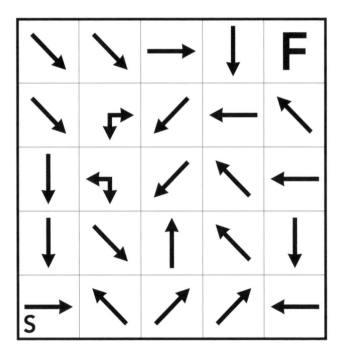

Cube Logic 4

Which of the four foldable patterns can be folded
to make the cube displayed?

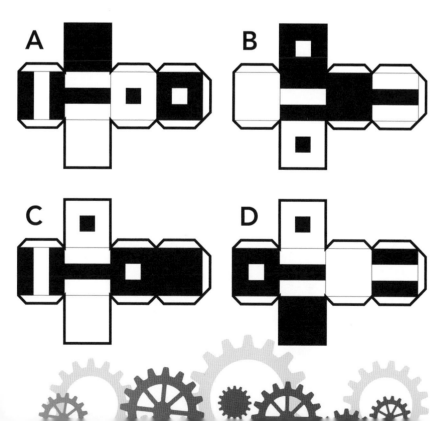

Tetra Grid 5

Drop each of the shapes into the grid in the order provided to spell ten six-letter words. Clues for the words have been provided next to the grid.

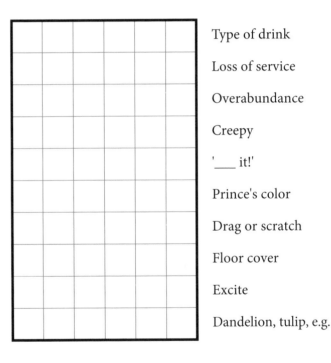

Type of drink

Loss of service

Overabundance

Creepy

'___ it!'

Prince's color

Drag or scratch

Floor cover

Excite

Dandelion, tulip, e.g.

Numcross 5

Use the provided clues to fill the grid with numbers. No entry may start with a 0.

A	B		C	D	E
F			G		
	H	I			
		J		K	
L	M			N	O
P				Q	

Across

A. D down + 6
C. A perfect square
F. A perfect cube
G. A trio of odd digits
H. 2 × J across
J. D down × 9
L. A palindrome
N. F across - 1
P. Consecutive digits in descending order
Q. The sum of the digits in G across

Down

A. Another perfect square
B. Another perfect square
C. 2 × G across
D. Another perfect square
E. Square root of C across
I. Feet in one mile
K. E down × M down
L. N across + 19
M. Q across in reverse
O. A down - 1

Pent Words 4

Split the grid into shapes, and use the clues provided to spell five-letter words across each row and within each shape. Shape clues include an outline, but the shape may be rotated or reflected.

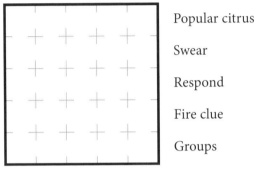

Popular citrus

Swear

Respond

Fire clue

Groups

 Coffee addition

 Sodas in Texas

 Sauna feature

Primate

Start

UFO Sighting 2

Use the clues provided to find five answers containing the letters UFO.

_ O U _ F _ _   Profound

F O U _ _ _   First non-medalist

F O _ U _   Clarity

F U _ O _   Intensity

F U _ O _   Convertible furniture piece

Arrow Maze 6

Each move, jump from your current square to another square in the same row, column, or diagonal as permitted by the arrow or arrows provided. There are no dead ends here. Can you get from Start to Finish in 10 steps?

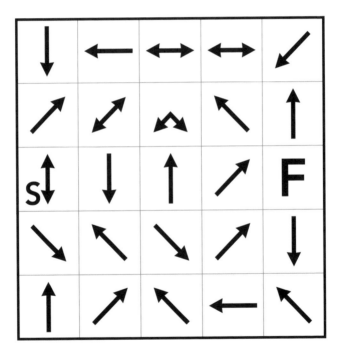

Word Sudoku 5

In the sudoku grid, enter one of each of six unique letters into each row, column, and boldly-outlined six-celled shape without repetition.

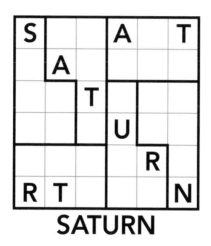

SATURN

Maze 4

In this maze, you may cross under paths using tunnels where indicated by arrows.

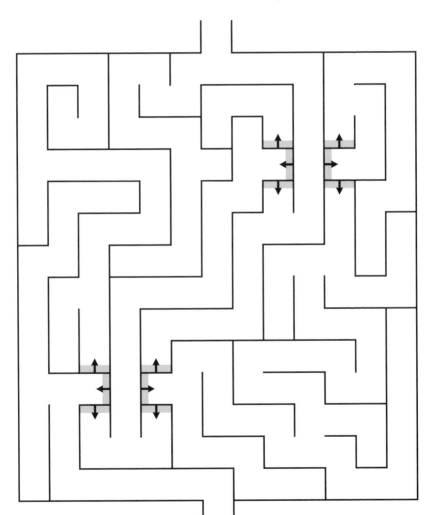

Symbol Sums 5

The sums of five combinations of symbols have been provided. What is the value of each individual symbol?

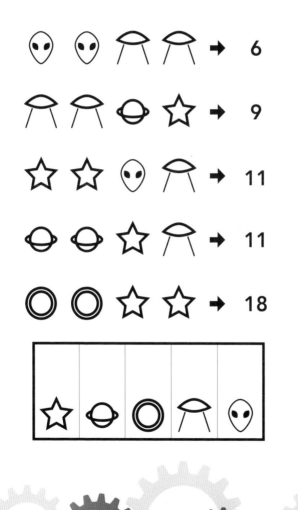

Story Logic 4

The author's cats are picky little jerks, and finding a catsitter is a pain. Use the clues to match the names to the cats' appearances, food preference, and the only place they will let you pet them.

		Description				Petting Spot				Food			
		Black, Green Eyes	Black, Orange Eyes	Gray and Large	Gray and Small	Back	Chin	Head	Neck	Beef Chunks	Beef Pâté	Chicken Cutlets	Flaked Tuna
Cat	Frankie												
	Nina Bean												
	Ruby												
	Sailor												
Food	Beef Chunks												
	Beef Pâté												
	Chicken Cutlets												
	Flaked Tuna												
Petting Spot	Back												
	Chin												
	Head												
	Neck												

Frankie and Ruby have black fur but different eye colors.

Neither of the gray-furred cats prefer being scratched under their necks.

One cat prefers both head scratches and beef pâté.

The cat with black fur and green eyes does not prefer flaked tuna.

Ruby prefers either neck or chin rubs.

Ruby and Sailor both prefer different kinds of beef.

Nina Bean prefers chicken cutlets and either enjoys back or head rubs.

The cat that prefers chin scratches loves beef chunks.

The big gray cat doesn't get along with the cat whose favorite food is chicken.

Rearrangement 7–8

Rearrange the letters in the phrase "KOALA DIRT" to spell a place where you might listen to banter about koalas.

Rearrange the letters in the phrase "A WILDER SET" to spell a ride some wild folks might take.

Tetra Grid 6

Drop each of the shapes into the grid in the order
provided to spell ten six-letter words. Clues for
the words have been provided next to the grid.

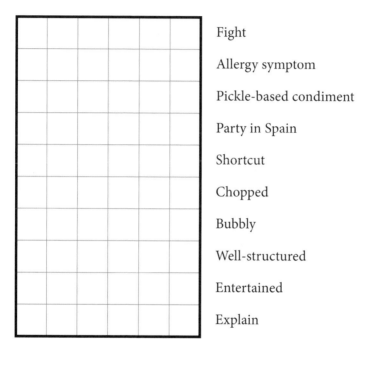

Fight

Allergy symptom

Pickle-based condiment

Party in Spain

Shortcut

Chopped

Bubbly

Well-structured

Entertained

Explain

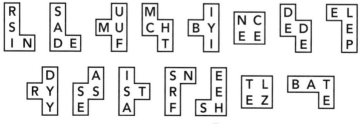

Numcross 6

Use the provided clues to fill the grid with numbers. No entry may start with a 0.

A	B	■	C	D	E
F		■	G		
H		I		■	■
■	■	J		K	L
M	N		■	O	
P			■	Q	

Across

- A. Square root of A down
- C. E down + K down
- F. A perfect square
- G. Digits that sum to 18
- H. Year of the debut of the movie Jurassic Park
- J. Year of the debut of the movie Jurassic World
- M. A palindrome
- O. 4 × A across
- P. L down - 300
- Q. Another perfect square

Down

- A. Another palindrome
- B. P across - 90
- C. C across × 10
- D. Another perfect square
- E. O across - 5
- I. Another palindrome
- K. Another perfect square
- L. 3 × C across
- M. 2 × A across
- N. A perfect cube

Pent Words 5

Split the grid into shapes, and use the clues provided to spell five-letter words across each row and within each shape. Shape clues include an outline, but the shape may be rotated or reflected.

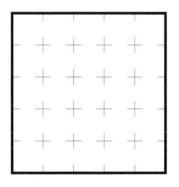

Suit

Sample

Ruffles chip feature

Groom

Small overlay

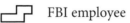 FBI employee

 Group of lions

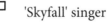 'Skyfall' singer

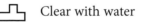 Clear with water

Comic instance

Cube Logic 5

Which of the four foldable patterns can be folded to make the cube displayed?

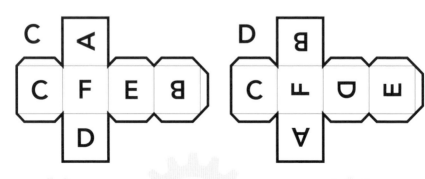

Symbol Sums 6

The sums of five combinations of symbols have been provided. What is the value of each individual symbol?

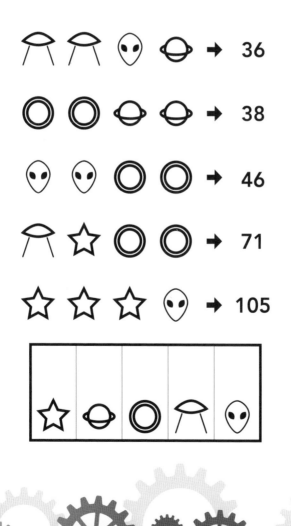

Arrow Maze 7

Each move, jump from your current square to another square in the same row, column, or diagonal as permitted by the arrow or arrows provided. There are no dead ends here. Can you get from Start to Finish in 10 steps?

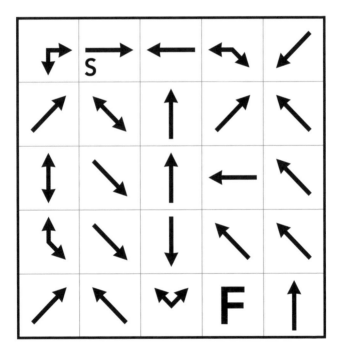

Word Sudoku 6

In the sudoku grid, enter one of each of six unique letters into each row, column, and boldly-outlined six-celled rectangle without repetition.

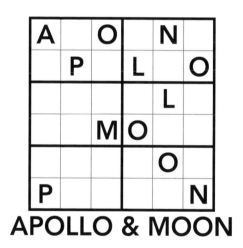

APOLLO & MOON

Numcross 7

Use the provided clues to fill the grid with numbers. No entry may start with a 0.

A	B	C		D	E	F		G	H
I				J				K	
	L	M				N	O		
P	Q					R			
S			T	U	V		W	X	Y
Z		AA		BB		CC		DD	
	EE	FF				GG	HH		
II	JJ			KK					
LL			MM	NN			OO	PP	QQ
RR			SS			TT			

Across

A. Name of a convenience store chain
D. A palindrome
G. A perfect cube
I. 2 × BB Across
J. Digits that sum to 10
K. One half of A down
L. J across × 2
N. Consecutive digits in ascending order
P. Another palindrome
R. DD across + 5
S. 2 × PP down
T. D down - 30
W. PP down × QQ down
Z. AA down in reverse
BB. W across - 100
DD. PP down in reverse
EE. U down + 10
GG. HH down × 2
II. Another palindrome
KK. BB across + 5
LL. QQ down × 2
MM. SS across + 1
OO. QQ down squared
RR. A perfect square
SS. L across × 2
TT. Anagram of OO across

Down

A. G across in reverse
B. Another perfect square
C. Consecutive digits in ascending order
D. D across - 8
E. PP down + 5
F. Consecutive digits in descending order
G. Consecutive digits in ascending order
H. Consecutive digits in descending order
M. X down in reverse
O. 3 × Y down
P. Another palindrome
Q. D across + 5
U. Another perfect square
V. K across in reverse
X. Anagram of W across
Y. BB across - 7
AA. U down × QQ down
CC. One fifth of H down
FF. P across + RR across
HH. MM across × 4
II. TT across × 2
JJ. 5 × RR across
KK. W across in reverse
NN. 5 × QQ down
PP. G across - 6
QQ. PP down - 10

Symbol Sums 7

The sums of five combinations of symbols have been provided. What is the value of each individual symbol?

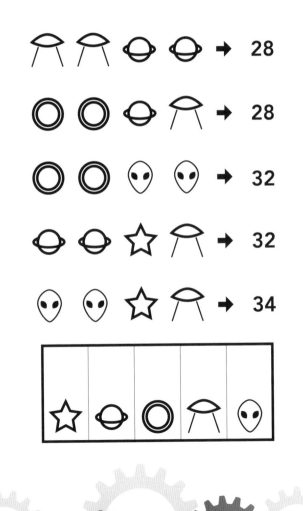

Tetra Grid 7

Drop each of the shapes into the grid in the order provided to spell ten six-letter words. Clues for the words have been provided next to the grid.

Popular puzzle game

Wooded area

Water down

Fried chicken vessel

Desert plant

Like corn at a theater

Water heater

Dealing with teeth

Purchase incentive

Pressed

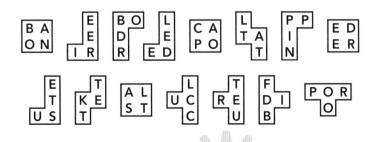

Pent Words 6

Split the grid into shapes, and use the clues provided to spell five-letter words across each row and within each shape. Shape clues include an outline, but the shape may be rotated or reflected.

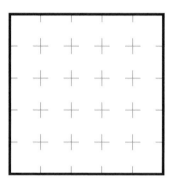

Common metal

Unit of an herb

Delta

Separate

Like some guacamole

Shindig

Teapot feature

Some puzzles in this book

Pilot

Visible energy

Cube Logic 6

Which of the four foldable patterns can be folded
to make the cube displayed?

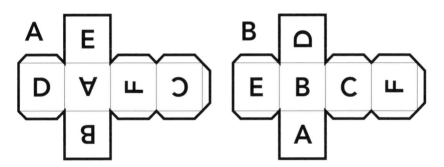

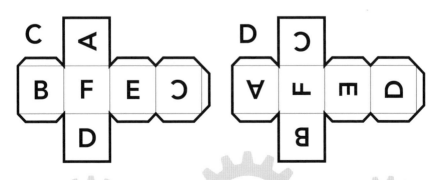

Story Logic 5

Corporate is restructuring and planning to have four divisions. Match the divisions with their time zone, leader, number of locations, and branding color.

		Time Zone				Branding Color				Locations			
		Pacific Time	Mountain Time	Central Time	Eastern Time	Blue	Green	Purple	Red	33 Locations	47 Locations	57 Locations	59 Locations
Leader	Kelsey												
	Lance												
	Myka												
	Nanette												
Locations	33 Locations												
	47 Locations												
	57 Locations												
	59 Locations												
Branding Color	Blue												
	Green												
	Purple												
	Red												

Mountain Time division has more locations than Pacific Time division.

Central Time division has more locations than Eastern Time division.

Kelsey's division has more locations than the one with purple branding.

The green-branded division has fewer locations than the purple-branded division.

The Pacific Time division has red branding.

Nanette's division does not have purple branding.

Kelsey's division has the most locations.

Myka's division is not located in Mountain Time.

Nanette's division is further west than both the division with 33 locations and than Myka's division.

The red-branded division has more locations than the purple-branded division.

Word Sudoku 7

In the sudoku grid, enter one of each of six unique letters into each row, column, and boldly-outlined six-celled rectangle without repetition.

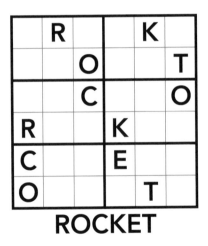

ROCKET

Arrow Maze 8

Each move, jump from your current square to another square in the same row, column, or diagonal as permitted by the arrow or arrows provided. There are no dead ends here. Can you get from Start to Finish in 9 steps?

→	→	↙	←	↙
↗	↖	S↗	↓	←
↕	←	↑	↘	↙
↗	←	F	→	↖
↑	↗	←	→	↑

Tetra Grid 8

Drop each of the shapes into the grid in the order provided to spell ten six-letter words. Clues for the words have been provided next to the grid.

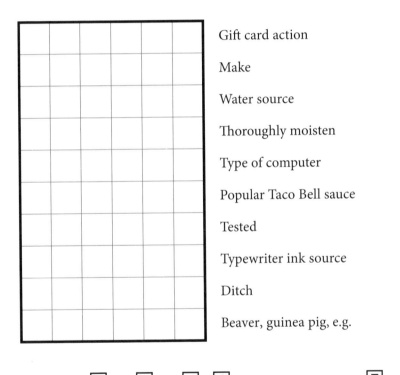

Gift card action

Make

Water source

Thoroughly moisten

Type of computer

Popular Taco Bell sauce

Tested

Typewriter ink source

Ditch

Beaver, guinea pig, e.g.

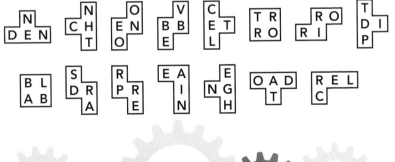

Rearrangement 9–10

Rearrange the letters in the phrase "PARKA WRESTLING" to spell something you might drink after a tough bout.

Rearrange the letters in the phrase "CATLIKE NOSTRILS" to spell something the author's cats might smell while he's cooking.

Ringed Planet 1

Use the clues to place six words, each six letters in length, around the planet. Words may go clockwise or counterclockwise as needed.

Chosen

Closed

Grouchy

Privateer

Sophisticated

Stacked

Symbol Sums 8

The sums of five combinations of symbols have been provided. What is the value of each individual symbol?

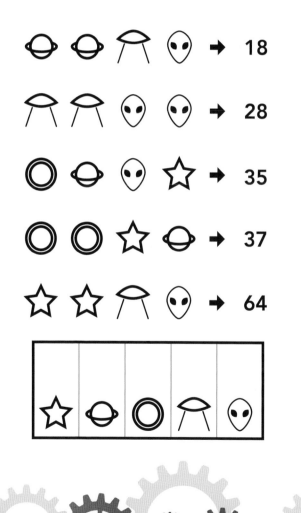

Cube Logic 7

Which of the four foldable patterns can be folded
to make the cube displayed?

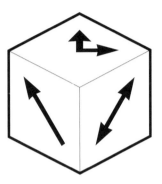

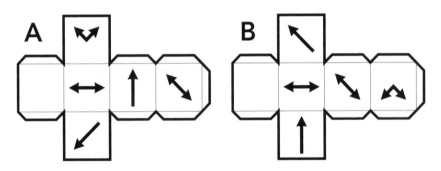

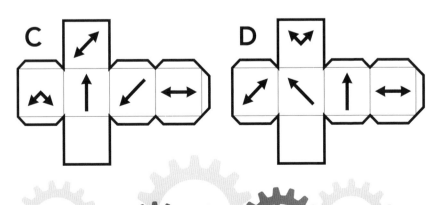

Pent Words 7

Split the grid into shapes, and use the clues provided to spell five-letter words across each row and within each shape. Shape clues include an outline, but the shape may be rotated or reflected.

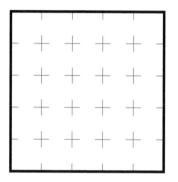

Craft

NASCAR Competitor

Beg

Oyster contents

A direction

 Quick-witted

Meteorologist's tool

 Outcast

Diet food descriptor

Tranquility

Numcross 8

Use the provided clues to fill the grid with numbers. No entry may start with a 0.

A	B		C	D		E	F	G	H
I		J				K			
L				M	N			O	
P			Q					R	
		S			T	U	V		
		W		X		Y			
Z	AA			BB	CC			DD	EE
FF			GG				HH		
II		JJ			KK	LL			
MM					NN			OO	

Across		Down	
A.	A famous 'secret' area	A.	Consecutive digits in
C.	C down + 1		ascending order
E.	One fifth of D down	B.	S across squared
I.	Contains every even	C.	A perfect cube
	digit: 0, 2, 4, 6, 8	D.	Anagram of CC down
K.	B down + D down	E.	EE down - E across
L.	A palindrome	F.	DD across in reverse
M.	Y across × OO across	G.	D down + 800
O.	A perfect square	H.	Another palindrome
P.	C down + 20	J.	Another perfect cube
Q.	Consecutive digits in	N.	Q across - 10
	descending order	Q.	Another perfect square
R.	O across + 10	S.	Another perfect square
S.	S down - 4	U.	T across - 20
T.	OO across squared	V.	OO across in reverse
W.	Q across + 1	X.	One half of B down
Y.	OO across + 1	Z.	AA down - 10
Z.	V down - 1	AA.	(E down × 10) + 6
BB.	Another palindrome	CC.	I across - KK across
DD.	Another perfect square	DD.	CC down + HH down
FF.	JJ down × 2	EE.	Another palindrome
GG.	U down in reverse	GG.	C down + DD across
HH.	Another palindrome	HH.	C down - J down
II.	Consecutive digits in	JJ.	Z across × 3
	ascending order	LL.	Another perfect square
KK.	Contains every odd		
	digit: 1, 3, 5, 7, 9		
MM.	G down - 10		
NN.	C down - 8		
OO.	HH down - LL down		

Arrow Maze 9

Each move, jump from your current square to another square in the same row, column, or diagonal as permitted by the arrow or arrows provided. There are no dead ends here. Can you get from Start to Finish in 9 steps?

Tetra Grid 9

Drop each of the shapes into the grid in the order provided to spell ten six-letter words. Clues for the words have been provided next to the grid.

Diluted

Mouse wheel action

Light coat/sweatshirt

Put into service

Plan

Farm dwellers

Data entry worker

Pizza cheese descriptor

Frequent salad pasta shape

Dresser feature

Word Sudoku 8

In the sudoku grid, enter one of each of six unique letters into each row, column, and boldly-outlined six-celled rectangle without repetition.

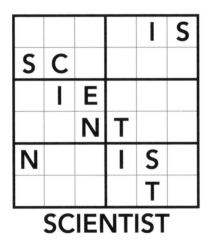

SCIENTIST

Symbol Sums 9

The sums of five combinations of symbols have been provided. What is the value of each individual symbol?

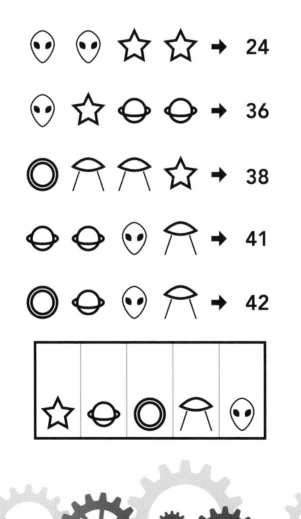

Story Logic 6

The big televised music competition is down to the semifinals! Use the clues to match the genre to the winner, second place, and third place!

		Winner				Second				Third			
		Jai	Keisha	Lindsey	Mac	Kirk	Lana	Mark	Nate	Sasha	Tess	Uma	Vick
Genre	Country												
	Hip-Hop												
	Pop												
	Rock												
Third	Sasha												
	Tess												
	Uma												
	Vick												
Second	Kirk												
	Lana												
	Mark												
	Nate												

Tess lost out to Jai.

Sasha and Kirk competed in the same genre.

Nate competed in either Pop or Rock, not against Uma.

Lana did not compete in the Hip-Hop genre.

Jai doesn't do Country.

Mac competed in Hip-Hop.

Uma competed in the same category as Lindsey or Mac.

Vick and Keisha did not compete against each other.

Sasha competed in either Hip-Hop or Rock.

Vick was beat by either Keisha or Lindsey.

Rearrangement 11–12

Rearrange the letters in the phrase "BOUNTY THERE" to spell something that ought to be applied bountifully to chicken biscuits.

Rearrange the letters in the phrase "REAR SEATS" to spell somewhere a passenger on a road trip could stretch their legs.

Cube Logic 8

Which of the four foldable patterns can be folded
to make the cube displayed?

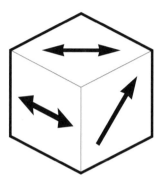

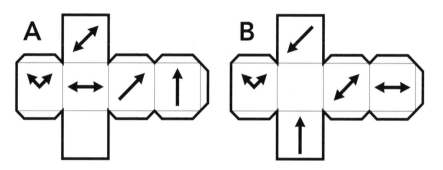

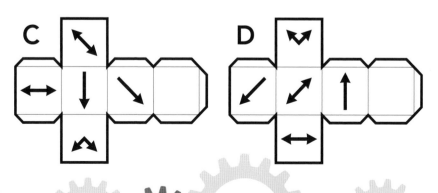

Arrow Maze 10

Each move, jump from your current square to another square in the same row, column, or diagonal as permitted by the arrow or arrows provided. There are no dead ends here. Can you get from Start to Finish in 8 steps?

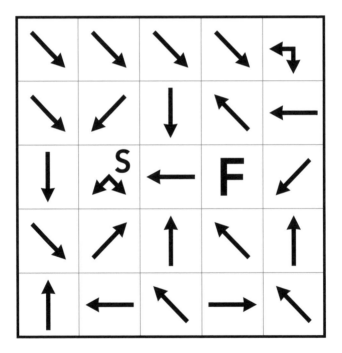

Rearrangement 13–14

Rearrange the letters in the phrase "CAVERNS RUINS" to spell something you need to prevent your computer from becoming ruinous.

Rearrange the letters in the phrase "BREAK MY SON" to spell some playground equipment that could cause an injury if used improperly.

Symbol Sums 10

The sums of five combinations of symbols have been provided. What is the value of each individual symbol?

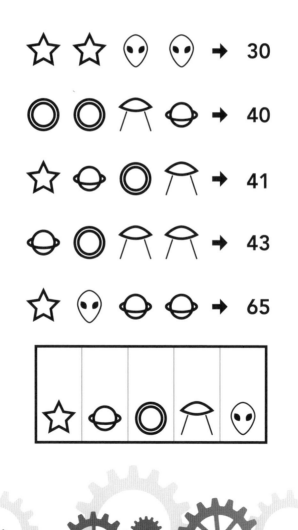

Pent Words 8

Split the grid into shapes, and use the clues
provided to spell five-letter words across each row
and within each shape. Shape clues include an
outline, but the shape may be rotated or reflected.

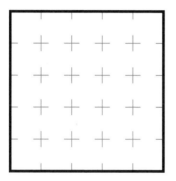

Buffalo

Type of bear

Betwixt

Old cinema contents

A digit

 Interpret

 Realm

 Like some RPG characters

Type of radar

Craves

Ringed Planet 2

Use the clues to place six words, each six letters in length, around the planet. Words may go clockwise or counterclockwise as needed.

City in Arizona

Less Happy

Manage

Marksman

Ruined Grape

Time Leading to Christmas

Rearrangement 15–16

Rearrange the letters in the phrase "SNARED IVY" to spell somewhere full of plants.

Rearrange the letters in the phrase "PUNKS CHOICE" to spell something even punks will eat when they're sick.

Word Sudoku 9

In the sudoku grid, enter one of each of six unique letters into each row, column, and boldly-outlined six-celled shape without repetition.

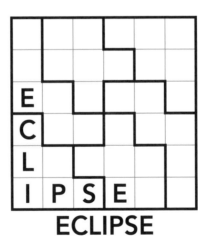

ECLIPSE

Cube Logic 9

Which of the four foldable patterns can be folded
to make the cube displayed?

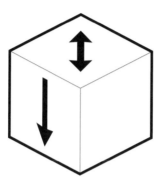

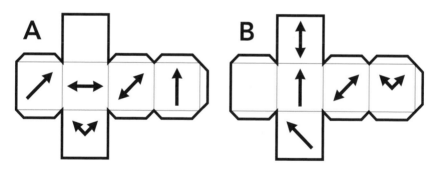

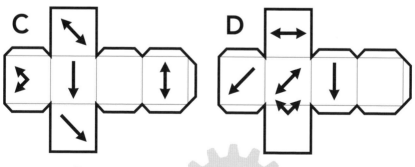

Ringed Planet 3

Use the clues to place six words, each six letters in length, around the planet. Words may go clockwise or counterclockwise as needed.

Back Teeth

Guard

Monetary Awards

Most Adorable

Root Vegetable

Sidearm

Symbol Sums 11

The sums of five combinations of symbols have been provided. What is the value of each individual symbol?

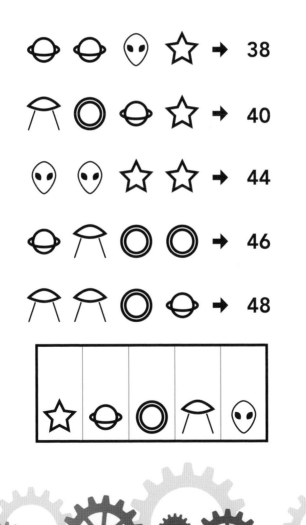

Story Logic 7

A family reunion and barbecue is planned for this summer. Use the clues to match each of the cousins with their occupation, the dish they brought, and how far away they live.

		Drive Time				Occupation				Dish			
		20 Minutes	32 Minutes	45 Minutes	57 Minutes	Cashier	Doctor	Firefighter	Mechanic	Cookies	Hot dish	Jello Mold	Pasta Salad
Cousin	Kayla												
	Lenore												
	Michael												
	Ned												
Dish	Cookies												
	Hot dish												
	Jello Mold												
	Pasta Salad												
Occupation	Cashier												
	Doctor												
	Firefighter												
	Mechanic												

Lenore, who lives closer than the doctor, brought her famous tater tot hot dish. You know, the casserole with the creamy soup and the French fried onions on top?

The cashier brought a savory dish to the barbecue.

Michael lives farther away than both the cousin that brought cookies and the one that brought pasta salad.

The cousin who brought a Jello mold lives farther away than the mechanic, and both of them live farther away than the cousin who works as a firefighter.

Kayla's drive was more than twice as long as Lenore's.

Ned, who does not work as a cashier, lives closer than the cousin who brought cookies.

Rearrangement 17–18

Rearrange the letters in the phrase "DEAR HOMELAND" to spell something the author drinks when back home in Michigan with friends.

Rearrange the letters in the phrase "ERASER TIP" to spell another item made of rubber.

Symbol Sums 12

The sums of five combinations of symbols have been provided. What is the value of each individual symbol?

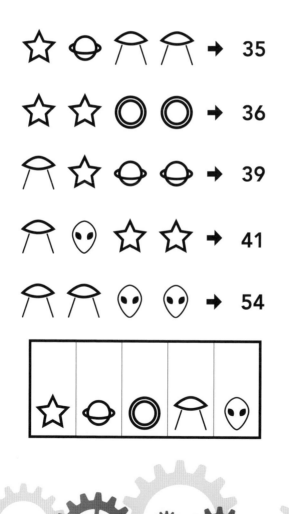

Cube Logic 10

Which of the four foldable patterns can be folded
to make the cube displayed?

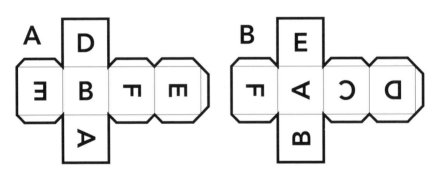

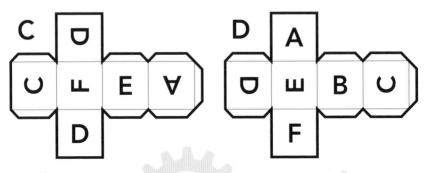

Rows Garden 1

Using the clues provided, enter a letter into each triangle to fill the garden. Each row contains one or two entries, and each hexagonal flower contains a six-letter word wrapped around the center. It's up to you to determine where to place the starting letter and the direction of the word.

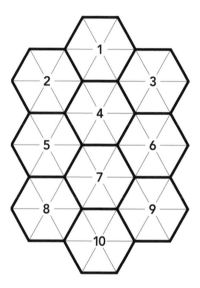

Surname to Scooby or Scrappy

Wrestler Rhodes/Glitzy accessories

Wrongful act/Creative

Dog treat/Chapman on OITNB

"Put a ___ on it!"/Multi-person race

Sara Quin's sis/Dairy producers

Fortune-telling cards/Ready

Everyone's MySpace friend

Flowers

1. With Mary, a drink
2. BBC sci-fi character
3. Greedy
4. Seafaring bandit
5. Oft-tied bit of cloth

6. Instant sports feature
7. Ballet performer
8. Bullseye
9. Arm joints
10. Red fruit

Black Holes 1

Divide the grid into chunks along the guides provided so that each chunk contains one black hole, and so the digits in the chunk sum to the number in the black hole.

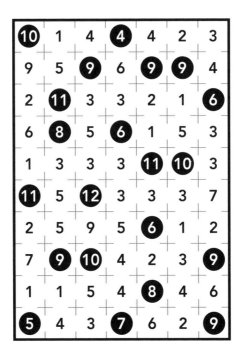

Chess Sudoku 1

Place a digit from 1 to 8 into each empty cell so that each row, column, and 3x3 block contains each digit once, without repetition. The chess knights in the grid display the sum of the digits in the cells which they can attack.

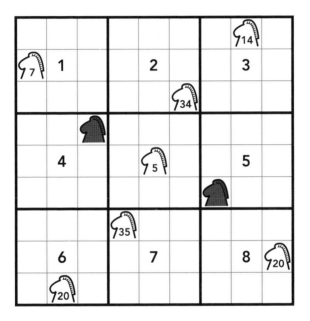

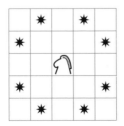

Story Logic 8

'Tis the season for trick-or-treating, and five locals are earning extra cash working at a haunted house. Use the clues to match each person with their haunted house section, the section's theme, and their costume.

		Section					Scene					Costume				
		Section 1	Section 2	Section 3	Section 4	Section 5	Cavern	Cemetery	Crypt	Jail	Sawmill	Goblin	Mummy	Skeleton	Vampire	Zombie
Employee	Jared															
	Kiera															
	Landon															
	Mekala															
	Nupur															
Costume	Goblin															
	Mummy															
	Skeleton															
	Vampire															
	Zombie															
Scene	Cavern															
	Cemetery															
	Crypt															
	Jail															
	Sawmill															

Landon's sawmill scene is somewhere after the scene with the employee in the goblin costume.

Nupur is not dressed as a skeleton or a zombie.

Jared, who works in the jail section, is not dressed in the vampire costume.

Kiera works in section number 2, which is either immediately before or after the cavern scene.

The crypt scene, whose employee is dressed as either a skeleton or a vampire, is before the goblin's scene.

Mekala works in the very first section.

The employee dressed as a mummy works exactly two sections after the jail scene.

The scene with the employee in the zombie costume is directly between the scenes with the vampire and in the cemetery, in some order.

Tetra Grid 10

Drop each of the shapes into the grid in the order provided to spell ten six-letter words. Clues for the words have been provided next to the grid.

Warm-colored metal

Talkative

Cool kitchen appliance

Infrequently

Family of fruits

Coffee-making utility

Utilitarian garment feature

Roadway

Mystery

Worst day of the week

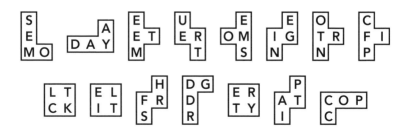

Symbol Sums 13

The sums of five combinations of symbols have been provided. What is the value of each individual symbol?

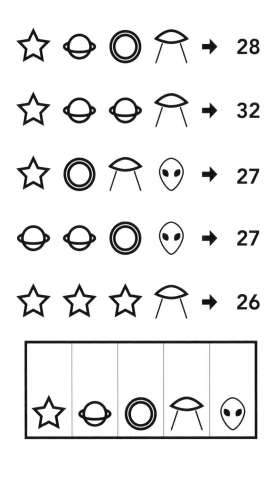

Numcross 9

Use the provided clues to fill the grid with numbers.
No entry may start with a 0.

A	B	C		D	E
F				G	
		H	I		
J	K				
L			M	N	O
P			Q		

Across

A. Emergency phone number in the US.

D. A down – O down

F. A perfect square

G. Another perfect square

H. J across + O down

J. D down × 5

L. O down – 10

M. Anagram of D down

P. D across – 1

Q. A multiple of 4

Down

A. Half of K down

B. Square root of F across

C. 2 ^ B down

D. Anagram of M across

E. A palindrome

I. Number whose digits sum to B down

J. Consecutive digits in ascending order

K. Part of the name of Tom DeLonge's band

N. 2 × O down

O. Teaspoons in 1 cup

Black Holes 2

Divide the grid into chunks along the guides
provided so that each chunk contains one black
hole, and so the digits in the chunk sum to the
number in the black hole.

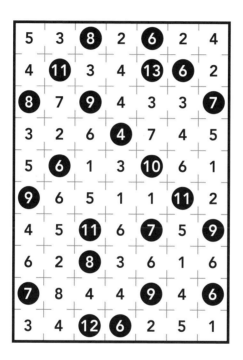

Rows Garden 2

Using the clues provided, enter a letter into each triangle to fill the garden. Each row contains one or two entries, and each hexagonal flower contains a six-letter word wrapped around the center. It's up to you to determine where to place the starting letter and the direction of the word.

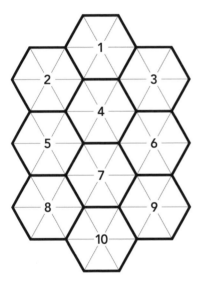

Plead

Dishonest person/Well-suited

Actor Welles/Make a cut

E.g. Superman/Striped animal

News magazine/Clay creature

Chef Lalli Music/Cut back

Ripped/Mistake

Snatch

Flowers

1. Span
2. Naval worker
3. Melatonin gland
4. Wonderful clock button
5. Loner

6. Small glass toy
7. Frozen dessert
8. Dangling horse lure
9. Reflective surface
10. Classic web ad format

Rearrangement 19–20

Rearrange the letters in the phrase "OFFICERS' FLEET" to spell a necessity for keeping caffeinated while on duty.

Rearrange the letters in the phrase "NO BANDIT BARMAN" to spell a crime-fighting duo.

Cube Logic 11

Which of the four foldable patterns can be folded to make the cube displayed?

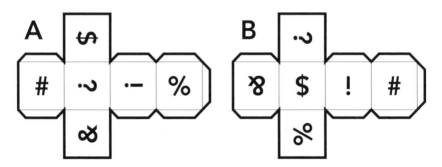

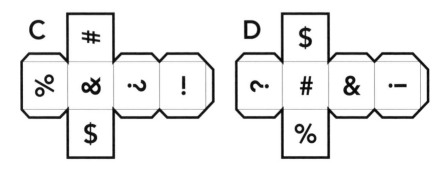

In Memoriam 1A

Memorize the names shown in the list below. When you're ready, turn the page and put your memory to the test.

Aubrey

Becky

Clara

Diedre

Eleanor

Felicia

Grant

Harish

Isabella

Jaspal

Kayla

Luis

Mason

In Memoriam 1B

Moving up, down, left, and right, make a path from
Start to Finish. You may only pass through squares
containing a name from the list on the previous page.

S	Harish	Kelly	Eleanor	Adria
Becky	Greta	Felicia	Aubrey	Grant
Luis	Diedre	Isabella	Louis	Mason
Irene	Kate	Jaspal	Ellen	Kayla
Claire	Didi	Clara	Joss	F

Tetra Grid 11

Drop each of the shapes into the grid in the order provided to spell ten six-letter words. Clues for the words have been provided next to the grid.

One of the Muppets

Savory fruit

Crunchy pad Thai topping

Building material

Take on

Party in Spain

Red suit

An ace in blackjack, often

Smart

NBC/ABC medical comedy

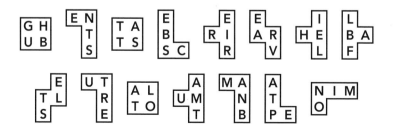

Story Logic 9

Trista's happy hour painting classes are getting scheduled for an upcoming week. Use the clues to match the night with the venue and the painting that will be taught in the class.

		Venue				Painting			
		Georgie's	The Brewery	The Tin Panther	Tres Amigas	Mountains	Sugar Skull	Sunset	Winter Scene
Evening	Sunday								
	Monday								
	Tuesday								
	Wednesday								
Painting	Mountains								
	Sugar Skull								
	Sunset								
	Winter Scene								

The class where a sunset will be painted is after the class at Tres Amigas.

The class at The Brewery is not the first or last class of this set of classes.

The painting of mountains, which will not take place at The Tin Panther, will be on Tuesday evening.

The painting of the wintery scene will either be at Georgie's or The Brewery.

The class at Georgie's will be before the class at The Brewery.

The class for the painting of the sugar skull will not take place at Tres Amigas.

The class teaching the wintery scene painting is set to take place before the class at The Tin Panther.

The painting of the sugar skull is not scheduled for Monday.

Black Holes 3

Divide the grid into chunks along the guides
provided so that each chunk contains one black
hole, and so the digits in the chunk sum to the
number in the black hole.

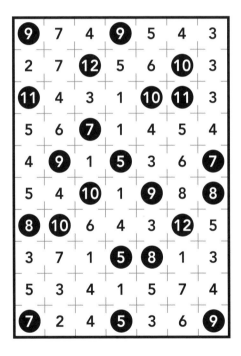

Rows Garden 3

Using the clues provided, enter a letter into each triangle to fill the garden. Each row contains one or two entries, and each hexagonal flower contains a six-letter word wrapped around the center. It's up to you to determine where to place the starting letter and the direction of the word.

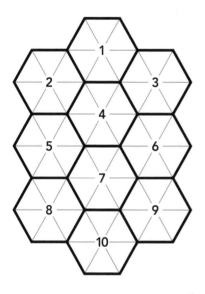

Grappler Anderson

Onlookers/Lack of difficulty

Genie location/Places to live

Antlered beast/First and last?

Farm structure/Garlic units

Hunk of metal/Industrial band

Ellen Pompeo role/E.g. Batman

Competed in a marathon

Flowers

1. Informed of danger
2. Uproar
3. Seed often used in food
4. Often-smart objects
5. Iconic robot vac brand

6. Finds at fault
7. Fastener
8. Spicy root
9. Repeated
10. Bird in a coal mine

Cube Logic 12

Which of the four foldable patterns can be folded to
make the cube displayed?

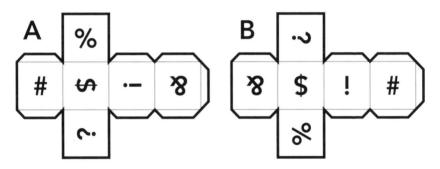

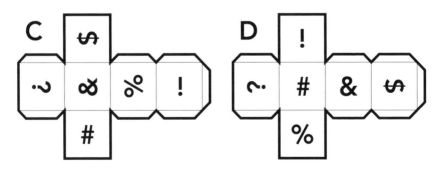

Numcross 10

Use the provided clues to fill the grid with numbers.
No entry may start with a 0.

A	B	■	C	D	E
F		■	G		
H		I		■	■
■		J		K	L
M	N		■	O	
P			■	Q	

Across

A. A perfect square
C. G across − P across
F. A across + 3
G. L down + 3
H. K down × F across
J. Contains every even digit except 0
M. A multiple of 7
O. Another perfect square
P. F across + O across
Q. Another perfect square

Down

A. E down + A across
B. 7 × E down
C. Consecutive digits in ascending order
D. A prime factor of E down
E. Balloons in Nena song
I. M across × 10
K. One-third of the sum of M across and P across
L. A palindrome
M. O across − 10
N. Q across + 4

Rearrangement 21–22

Rearrange the letters in the phrase "A CORRIDOR'S SIGNAL" to spell a location where you might find a traffic signal.

Rearrange the letters in the phrase "TRENDY HILARITY" to spell a location on a football field where a viral video of a goofy team mascot might be taken.

Symbol Sums 14

The sums of five combinations of symbols have been
provided. What is the value of each individual symbol?

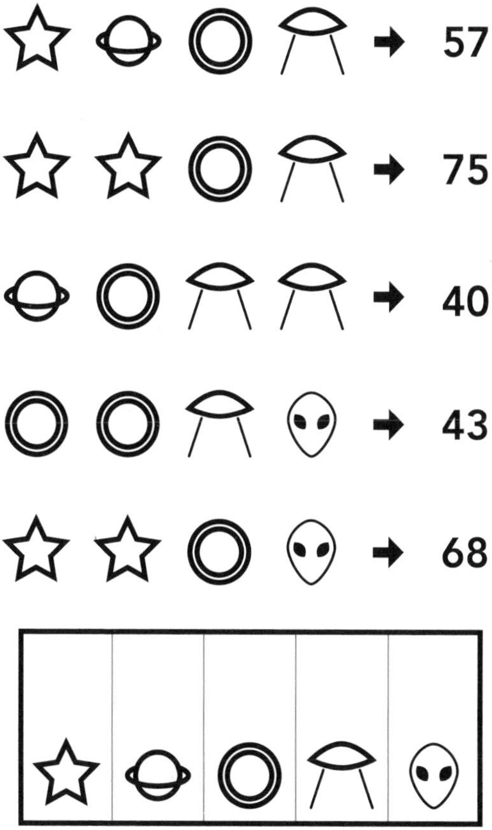

☆ ♄ ◎ ⏛ ➜ **57**

☆ ☆ ◎ ⏛ ➜ **75**

♄ ◎ ⏛ ⏛ ➜ **40**

◎ ◎ ⏛ 👽 ➜ **43**

☆ ☆ ◎ 👽 ➜ **68**

☆	♄	◎	⏛	👽

Tetra Grid 12

Drop each of the shapes into the grid in the order provided to spell ten six-letter words. Clues for the words have been provided next to the grid.

Natural water source

Bolt or screw partner

Random knowledge

Potential movie edible

Plant baby

Earlyish meal

Awfully chilly

Dee Dee's brother with a lab

German neighbor

Like some old film

Black Holes 4

Divide the grid into chunks along the guides provided so that each chunk contains one black hole, and so the digits in the chunk sum to the number in the black hole.

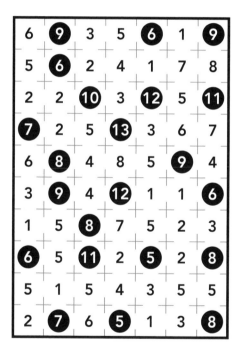

Chess Sudoku 2

Place a digit from 1 to 8 into each empty cell so that each row, column, and 3x3 block contains each digit once, without repetition. The chess knights in the grid display the sum of the digits in the cells which they can attack.

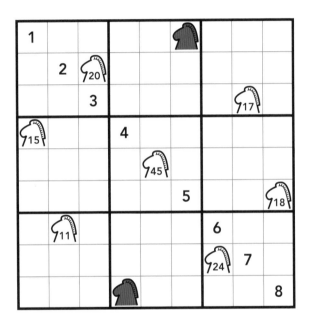

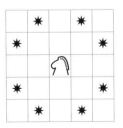

Numcross 11

Use the provided clues to fill the grid with numbers.
No entry may start with a 0.

A	**B**	**C**	■	**D**	**E**
F			■	**G**	
■		**H**	**I**		
J	**K**			■	■
L		■	**M**	**N**	**O**
P		■	**Q**		

Across

A. A palindrome
D. A perfect square
F. One-third of H across
G. Another perfect square
H. A down in binary
J. F across + I down
L. B down + N down
M. 2 × F across
P. One-third of A across
Q. An anagram of D down

Down

A. B down – 3
B. Another perfect square
C. An anagram of I down
D. A multiple of O down
E. Comedy Central series Reno ____
I. Digits that sum to A down
J. A down × 11
K. Consecutive digits in
    ascending order
N. D down / B down
O. A&E series The First ____

Rows Garden 4

Using the clues provided, enter a letter into each triangle to fill the garden. Each row contains one or two entries, and each hexagonal flower contains a six-letter word wrapped around the center. It's up to you to determine where to place the starting letter and the direction of the word.

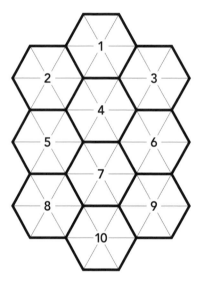

Dedicated creation

Trolley/Criminally smooth

Outbuilding/Push away

Local area or witch/wizard skills

Fad diet/Celestial bodies

Rifle type/Perform like Jay-Z

TV or internet medium/Air out

Former soldier

Flowers

1. Some photo subjects
2. Valentine's Day shapes
3. Preserve in brine
4. Pleasantly unreal
5. Paper for a speeder
6. Cuban exports
7. Share like a meme
8. Woodland dwellings
9. Mom or dad
10. Fuzzy fabric

In Memoriam 2A

Memorize the names shown in the list below. When you're ready, turn the page and put your memory to the test.

Fred

George

Harry

Joey

John

Monica

Paul

Phoebe

Ringo

In Memoriam 2B

Moving up, down, left, and right, make a path from
Start to Finish. You may only pass through squares
containing a name from the list on the previous page.

S	George	Joey	John	Ginny
Rachel	Paul	Ron	Ross	Monica
John	Ringo	Harry	Rachel	Joey
Ross	Chandler	Fred	Ginny	George
Ron	Chandler	Monica	Phoebe	**F**

Symbol Sums 15

The sums of five combinations of symbols have been
provided. What is the value of each individual symbol?

☆ 🪐 ◎ 🛸 → 21

☆ ◎ 🛸 🛸 → 24

☆ 🪐 🪐 👽 → 23

🪐 ◎ ◎ 👽 → 28

🪐 🪐 🛸 👽 → 29

Cube Logic 13

Which of the four foldable patterns can be folded to make the cube displayed?

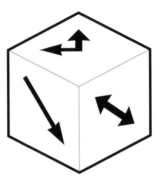

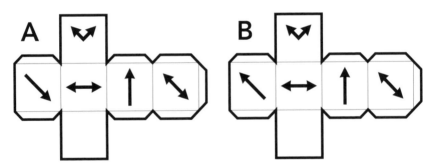

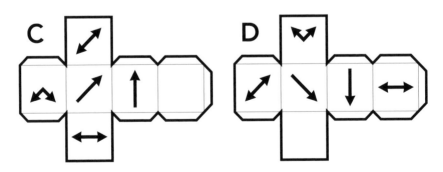

Rearrangement 23–24

Rearrange the letters in the phrase "LOCAL RESTORERS" to spell some attractions that likely require on-site mechanics.

Rearrange the letters in the phrase "ANNEXED ASPHALT" to spell a part of the United States where historic Route 66 once ran.

Black Holes 5

Divide the grid into chunks along the guides provided so that each chunk contains one black hole, and so the digits in the chunk sum to the number in the black hole.

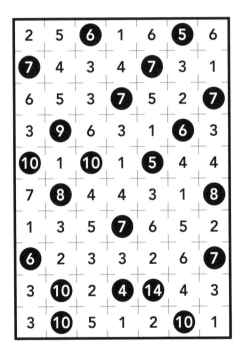

Tetra Grid 13

Drop each of the shapes into the grid in the order provided to spell ten six-letter words. Clues for the words have been provided next to the grid.

Item found above sinks

A bean variety

Flat and clear

Symmetrical shape

Empty

Dairy product

Straightforward

Laminated dough pastry

Do some sightseeing

Post office wares

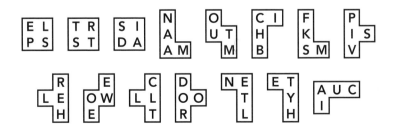

Numcross 12

Use the provided clues to fill the grid with numbers.
No entry may start with a 0.

A	B		C	D	E
F			G		
H		I			
		J		K	L
M	N			O	
P				Q	

Across

A.   One-third of F across

C.   A perfect square

F.   J across / C across

G.   Consecutive digits in ascending order

H.   An anagram of C down

J.   A palindrome

M.   8 × M down

O.   2 × F across

P.   Another palindrome

Q.   Another perfect square

Down

A.   Another perfect square

B.   Digits that sum to N down

C.   2 × P across

D.   Another perfect square

E.   No Doubt single

I.   Consecutive digits in ascending order

K.   L down – 3

L.   P across – M across

M.   A perfect cube

N.   Square root of C across

Symbol Sums 16

The sums of five combinations of symbols have been provided. What is the value of each individual symbol?

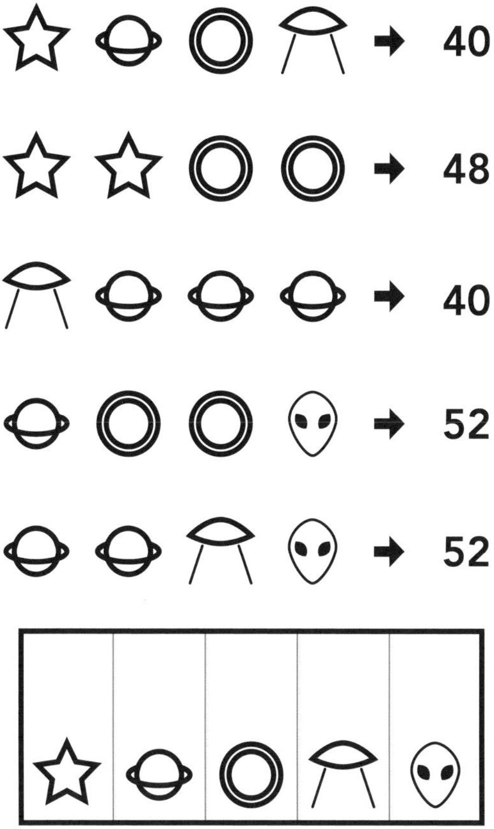

☆ ♄ ◎ ⛾ → **40**

☆ ☆ ◎ ◎ → **48**

⛾ ♄ ♄ ♄ → **40**

♄ ◎ ◎ 👽 → **52**

♄ ♄ ⛾ 👽 → **52**

☆	♄	◎	⛾	👽

Rows Garden 5

Using the clues provided, enter a letter into each
triangle to fill the garden. Each row contains one or
two entries, and each hexagonal flower contains a
six-letter word wrapped around the center. It's up to
you to determine where to place the starting letter
and the direction of the word.

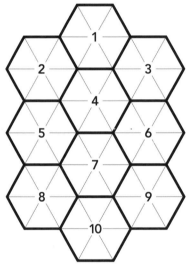

Mighty Mighty Bosstones' genre

Cause harm/Unusual

Center/War machines

Having enthusiasm/"High" shoes

Shaker contents/Strain

Famous twins/E.g. Coke, Pepsi

Baby cow/Partner to "Lost"

Frozen liquid

Flowers

1. Minor adjustments
2. Fried dough treat
3. Bar products
4. Made/kept warm
5. Mouth liquids
6. Arm covering
7. Engine or pump part
8. Folks from nearby
9. Money in London
10. Workplace

Cube Logic 14

Which of the four foldable patterns can be folded to make the cube displayed?

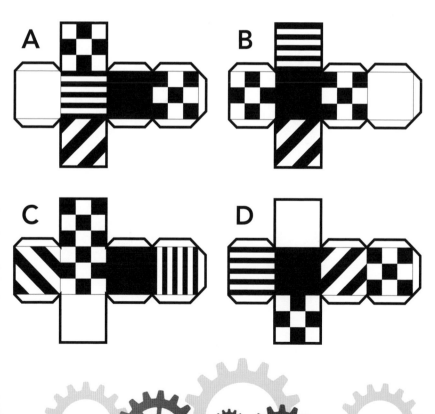

Chess Sudoku 3

Place a digit from 1 to 8 into each empty cell so that each row, column, and 3x3 block contains each digit once, without repetition. The chess knights in the grid display the sum of the digits in the cells which they can attack.

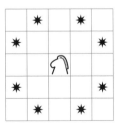

Rearrangement 25–26

Rearrange the letters in the phrase "DARN EAR AGAIN" to spell the name of a pop singer whose concerts might leave your ears ringing.

Rearrange the letters in the phrase "EASE OUT KITCHEN" to spell an option for dinner when you don't want to cook.

Tetra Grid 14

Drop each of the shapes into the grid in the order
provided to spell ten six-letter words. Clues for the
words have been provided next to the grid.

Colorful autumn sight

Oft-butterflied protein

E.g. Ronald, for McDonalds

Motivated

Adult beverage

Permanent decoration

Grown

Merchant

A connector of places

Rocky road covering

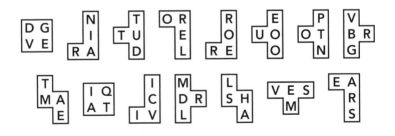

Numcross 13

Use the provided clues to fill the grid with numbers.
No entry may start with a 0.

	A	B	C		D	E
	F				G	
			H	I		
	J	K				
	L			M	N	O
	P			Q		

Across

A. 5 × F across

D. O down + 7

F. An anagram of K down

G. D across + 6

H. Contains one of every even digit except 0

J. Year US was founded

L. Sum of the digits in J across

M. Digits that sum to P across

P. A perfect square

Q. A palindrome

Down

A. Another perfect square

B. Another perfect square

C. (2 × H across) − 1

D. Consecutive digits in ascending order

E. Classic "page not found" error code

I. Q across × 11

J. Another perfect square

K. One-fourth of H across

N. A down + 7

O. L across + P across

Cube Logic 15

Which of the four foldable patterns can be folded to make the cube displayed?

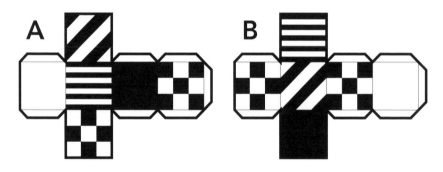

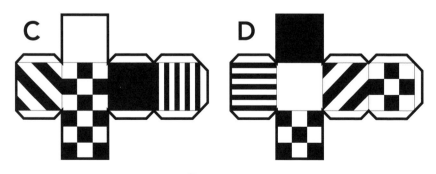

Black Holes 6

Divide the grid into chunks along the guides
provided so that each chunk contains one black
hole, and so the digits in the chunk sum to the
number in the black hole.

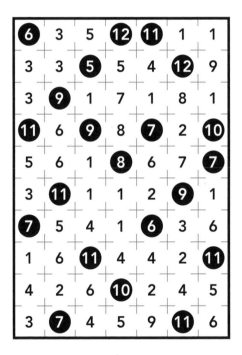

Story Logic 10

A hiking trail at the park is being created. Five new bridges are being added, each at various places along the trail and of different lengths. Use the clues to match the bridge specs with the notable people to which each bridge is dedicated.

		Mile Marker					Bridge Length				
		2.5 miles	2.7 miles	8.1 miles	8.3 miles	9.0 miles	20 feet	32 feet	40 feet	48 feet	60 feet
Dedication	David Biedny										
	Guy Fieri										
	Becky Lynch										
	Leah Remini										
	Adam Savage										
Bridge Length	20 feet					
	32 feet					
	40 feet					
	48 feet					
	60 feet					

The bridge dedicated to David Biedny is the last bridge on the trail.

The longest and shortest bridges are within one mile of each other.

The bridge dedicated to Adam Savage is more than one mile further along the trail than the 60-foot bridge.

The length of the bridge dedicated to Guy Fieri is exactly twice the length of the one dedicated to Leah Remini.

The 32-foot bridge is located at mile marker 8.3.

The bridge dedicated to Leah Remini is not the first bridge along the trail.

Numcross 14

Use the provided clues to fill the grid with numbers.
No entry may start with a 0.

A	**B**	■	**C**	**D**	**E**
F		■	**G**		
H		**I**		■	■
■	■	**J**		**K**	**L**
M	**N**		■	**O**	
P			■	**Q**	

Across

A. D down + 1
C. A perfect square
F. M down − 4
G. E down × Q across
H. An anagram of I down
J. B down × F across
M. Half of L down
O. N down − 3
P. Consecutive digits in ascending order
Q. 4 × D down

Down

A. Consecutive digits in ascending order
B. F across × 4
C. Start to many toll-free phone numbers
D. 2 × E down
E. Sum of digits in L down
I. Stephen King hotel room thriller
K. B down + G across
L. 5 × B down
M. Another perfect square
N. A perfect cube

Rearrangement 27–28

Rearrange the letters in the phrase "ENCHANT BIGWIG" to spell something that will take place if a TV executive greenlights a great new series.

Rearrange the letters in the phrase "EXACT MONIES" to spell a scenario where precision is very important.

Symbol Sums 17

The sums of five combinations of symbols have been provided. What is the value of each individual symbol?

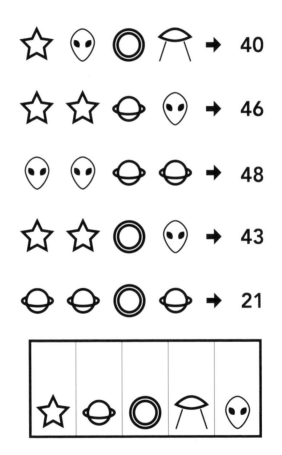

Tetra Grid 15

Drop each of the shapes into the grid in the order
provided to spell ten six-letter words. Clues for the
words have been provided next to the grid.

Mistake remover

Visit again

Tony organism

A Pacific coast state

Famed chain of "Houses"

Metric units of distance

Bring back

Significant timespan

Waxy light source

Heartbreaking

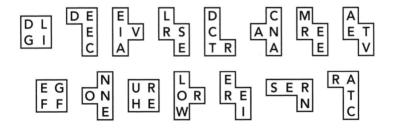

Black Holes 7

Divide the grid into chunks along the guides provided so that each chunk contains one black hole, and so the digits in the chunk sum to the number in the black hole.

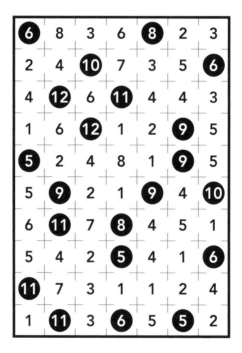

Numcross 15

Use the provided clues to fill the grid with numbers.
No entry may start with a 0.

A	B			C	D
E			F		
	G	H			
		I		J	
K	L			M	N
O				P	

Across

A.   A down – 1

C.   Sum of the digits in E and F across

E.   C across + C down

F.   A across × 3

G.   O across × C across

I.   M across + 10

K.   C across × K down

M.   L down + E across

O.   C down in reverse

P.   N down + 30

Down

A.   2 × O across

B.   C across × C down

C.   C across + 1

D.   C across + 2

F.   C across × 10

H.   3 × I across

J.   L down × 7

K.   4 × D down

L.   P across – 8

N.   A perfect square

Cube Logic 16

Which of the four foldable patterns can be folded to
make the cube displayed?

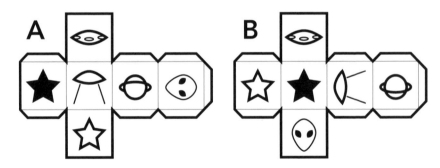

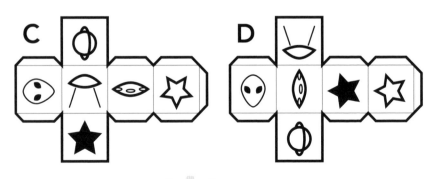

Rearrangement 29–30

Rearrange the letters in the phrase "IT'S ADORATION" to spell a way to hear your favorite band's music.

Rearrange the letters in the phrase "CLEAN GILLS" to spell what you need in order to post fishing trip photos online.

Symbol Sums 18

The sums of five combinations of symbols have been provided. What is the value of each individual symbol?

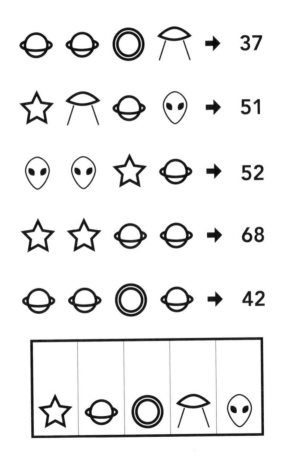

Tetra Grid 16

Drop each of the shapes into the grid in the order provided to spell ten six-letter words. Clues for the words have been provided next to the grid.

Popular type of drink

Close

Seasoned

A phase of matter

Conclude prematurely

Dire

Wood-based cooker

Iconic yellow Pixar character

Hair stylist

Like some inbox contents

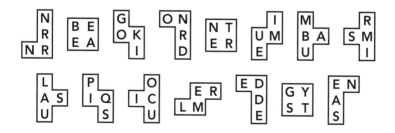

Rows Garden 6

Using the clues provided, enter a letter into each triangle to fill the garden. Each row contains one or two entries, and each hexagonal flower contains a six-letter word wrapped around the center. It's up to you to determine where to place the starting letter and the direction of the word.

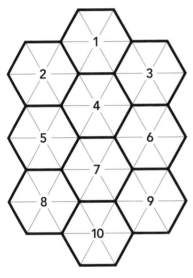

Term of endearment

Hot/Flying toy

Try again/Competitor

Apple part/Garden statue

Edit letter space/Common liquid

Cyclist activity/___ Lanka

Smoothie verb/Amazon device

Make a mistake

Flowers

1. Like some hearty soups
2. 8-legged creature
3. Orate
4. Citrus fruit
5. E.g. Ozzy, Dave Grohl
6. Far away
7. Outdoor partial cover
8. Dry pet food
9. Performing groups
10. Cook down some fat

Black Holes 8

Divide the grid into chunks along the guides provided so that each chunk contains one black hole, and so the digits in the chunk sum to the number in the black hole.

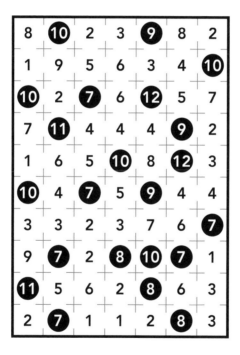

Story Logic 11

This year the local vegan cheezemonger society had its first annual vegan cheeze competition, and the results are in! Use the clues to match the recipe to its author and where their cheeze placed in the standings.

		Award					Cheeze Recipe				
		First Place	Second Place	Third Place	Fourth Place	Fifth Place	Carrot Cheddar	Cauliflower Queso	Nooch-Oh Sauce	Smoked Almond	Walnut Gouda
Cheezemonger	Amy										
	Breighdynn										
	Carol										
	Dirk										
	Eileen										
Cheeze Recipe	Carrot Cheddar										
	Cauliflower Queso										
	Nooch-Oh Sauce										
	Smoked Almond										
	Walnut Gouda										

Neither Carol nor Eileen made Cheezy Cauliflower Queso Dip.

Dirk's recipe placed in the bottom three.

Dirk's cheeze did better than both the Smoked Almond Cheeze Ball and the Cheezy Cauliflower Queso Dip.

The Wild Garlic Walnut Gouda Spread ranked higher than Eileen's recipe, which ranked higher than the recipe for the Smoked Almond Cheeze Ball.

Breighdynn's recipe placed somewhere in the top three.

The Carrot Cheddar Chunks were ranked higher than the recipe presented by Dirk.

Amy did not make the Carrot Cheddar Chunks.

The "Nooch-oh" Cheeze Sauce (featuring "nooch," the nickname of nutritional yeast) placed immediately between Carol's recipe and the recipe for the Carrot Cheddar Chunks in the standings.

Eileen, who did not make the Nooch-oh Cheeze Sauce, ranked either right ahead or behind Breighdynn's recipe in the standings.

Rearrangement 31–32

Rearrange the letters in the phrase "PATINA SCORN" to spell an item that requires a good coat of seasoning before use.

Rearrange the letters in the phrase "TRACTOR IMMUNE" to spell what you might ride to work if you switched from farming to a city job.

Cube Logic 17

Which of the four foldable patterns can be folded to make the cube displayed?

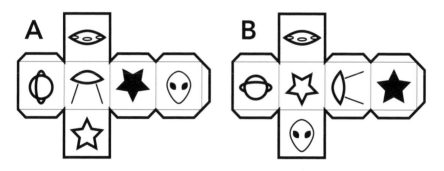

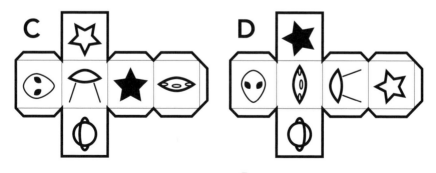

Tetra Grid 17

Drop each of the shapes into the grid in the order provided to spell ten six-letter words. Clues for the words have been provided next to the grid.

NASCAR competitor

Northerner

Woman dating young men

Frying noise

Sharpie product

Part of the US Congress

Sneak attack

Photographer's tool

Group of five letters

Doctrine

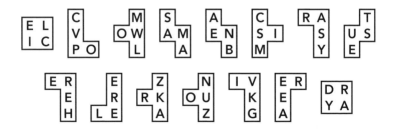

Symbol Sums 19

The sums of five combinations of symbols have been provided. What is the value of each individual symbol?

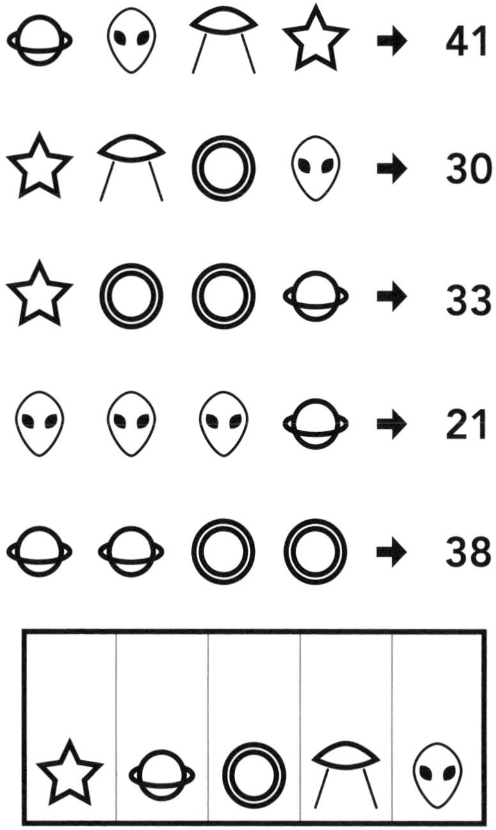

🪐 👽 🛸 ⭐ ➡ 41

⭐ 🛸 ◎ 👽 ➡ 30

⭐ ◎ ◎ 🪐 ➡ 33

👽 👽 👽 🪐 ➡ 21

🪐 🪐 ◎ ◎ ➡ 38

⭐	🪐	◎	🛸	👽

Black Holes 9

Divide the grid into chunks along the guides
provided so that each chunk contains one black
hole, and so the digits in the chunk sum to the
number in the black hole.

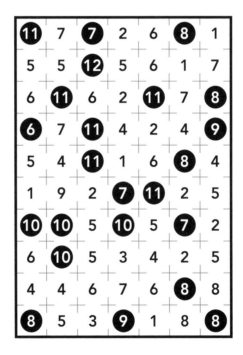

In Memoriam 3A

Memorize the numbers shown in the list below.
When you're ready, turn the page and put your
memory to the test.

Three

Six

Eight

Thirteen

Sixteen

Eighteen

Twenty-two

Twenty-four

Twenty-six

Twenty-eight

Thirty

In Memoriam 3B

Moving up, down, left, and right, make a path from
Start to Finish. You may only pass through squares
containing a number from the list on the previous page.

S	18	16	26	13
3	32	11	22	2
24	21	25	20	6
13	28	8	5	18
10	38	6	30	F

Numcross 16

Use the provided clues to fill the grid with numbers.
No entry may start with a 0.

A	B	░	░	C	D
E		F	░	G	
░	░	H	I		
J	K			░	░
L		░	M	N	O
P		░	░	Q	

Across

A. C across – B down

C. I down – J down

E. A down × 3

G. A across + 5

H. J across – (13 × L across)

J. D down × (B down + L across)

L. Sum of the digits in O down

M. A across × 6

P. B down × 2

Q. O down + L across

Down

A. N down in reverse

B. L across + 1

C. D down + K down

D. Unique digits that sum to 17, in ascending order

F. Consecutive digits in descending order

I. N down × P across

J. O down × 8

K. I down + 8

N. A perfect cube

O. Another perfect cube

Chess Sudoku 4

Place a digit from 1 to 8 into each empty cell so that each row, column, and 3x3 block contains each digit once, without repetition. The chess knights in the grid display the sum of the digits in the cells which they can attack.

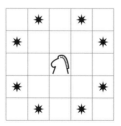

Symbol Sums 20

The sums of five combinations of symbols have been provided. What is the value of each individual symbol?

🪐 ☆ 🛸 ◎ → 61

◎ 🛸 👽 ☆ → 64

◎ 👽 👽 🪐 → 45

☆ ☆ ☆ 🪐 → 26

🪐 🪐 👽 👽 → 38

☆	🪐	◎	🛸	👽

Rearrangement 33–34

Rearrange the letters in the phrase "LATCHES SETUP" to spell a vehicle that likely has a lot of intricate parts.

Rearrange the letters in the phrase "DEFTEST HEIST" to spell what a robber might encounter if they mistook a linen closet for a bank vault.

Rows Garden 7

Using the clues provided, enter a letter into each triangle to fill the garden. Each row contains one or two entries, and each hexagonal flower contains a six-letter word wrapped around the center. It's up to you to determine where to place the starting letter and the direction of the word.

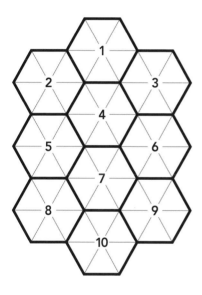

Food container

Like Randy Savage/College tests

Benefit/Desert refuge

Dance or sauce/Zelda protagonist

Artist Salvador/Brave

Nut used in pies/Dedicated

Logician Turing/Smooth move

"Want Ad" acronym

Flowers

1. Chips and cheese
2. Vacation vehicle, often
3. Inactive state
4. Fuzzy Australian "bears"
5. North Texas city

6. Pungent
7. Reptile
8. Royal home or mansion
9. Split apart
10. Not winning

Cube Logic 18

Which two of the six foldable patterns can be folded
to make the same cube?

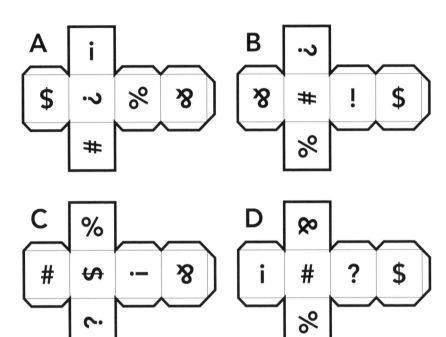

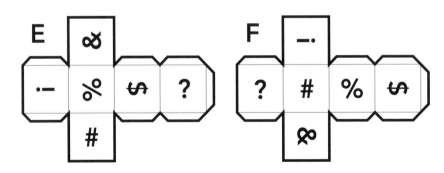

Black Holes 10

Divide the grid into chunks along the guides
provided so that each chunk contains one black
hole, and so the digits in the chunk sum to the
number in the black hole.

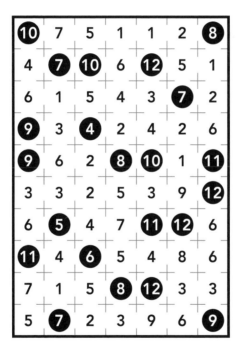

Symbol Sums 21

The sums of five combinations of symbols have been provided. What is the value of each individual symbol?

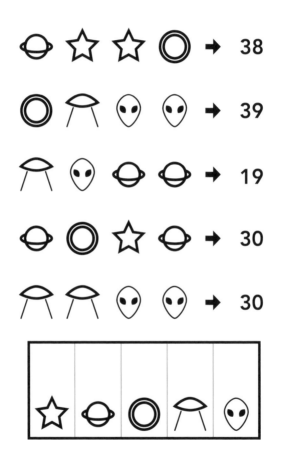

Tetra Grid 18

Drop each of the shapes into the grid in the order provided to spell ten six-letter words. Clues for the words have been provided next to the grid.

Actor's material

Golf location

Small, quick dinosaur

Convent occupant

Jewelry with storage

Live broadcast

Earned prize

A rainbow color

Format

Air pocket

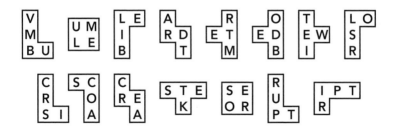

Numcross 17

Use the provided clues to fill the grid with numbers.
No entry may start with a 0.

A	B			C	D
E		F		G	
		H	I		
	J				
K			L	M	N
O				P	

Across

A. A perfect square

C. D down × 2

E. A down × 3

G. Another perfect square

H. L across + N down

J. P across × 4

K. Another perfect square

L. Another perfect square

O. 3 × K across

P. K down + 4

Down

A. C across – N down

B. Digits that sum to N down

C. A multiple of G across

D. A across – M down

F. C across × 6

I. N down × P across

J. P across × 5

K. A perfect cube

M. A across – D down

N. Square root of L across

Chess Sudoku 5

Place a digit from 1 to 8 into each empty cell so that each row, column, and 3x3 block contains each digit once, without repetition. The chess knights in the grid display the sum of the digits in the cells which they can attack.

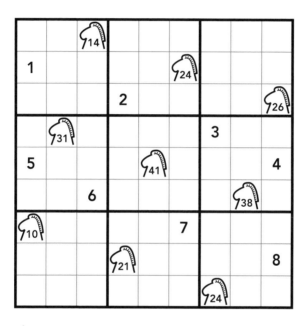

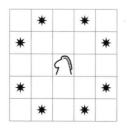

Tetra Grid 19A

Drop each of the shapes into the grid in the order provided to spell ten different six-letter words. In lieu of clues, these words form partial recipes.

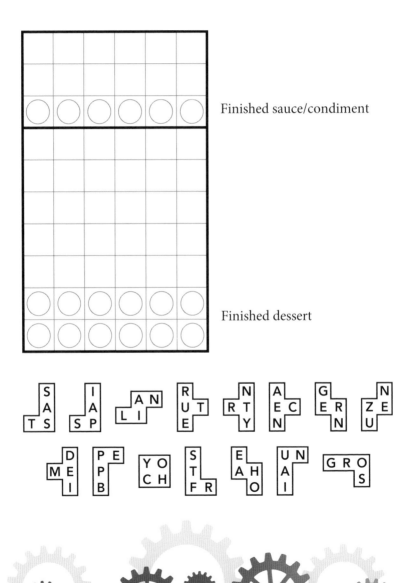

Finished sauce/condiment

Finished dessert

Tetra Grid 19B

Drop each of the shapes into the grid in the order provided to spell ten different six-letter words. In lieu of clues, these words form a partial recipe.

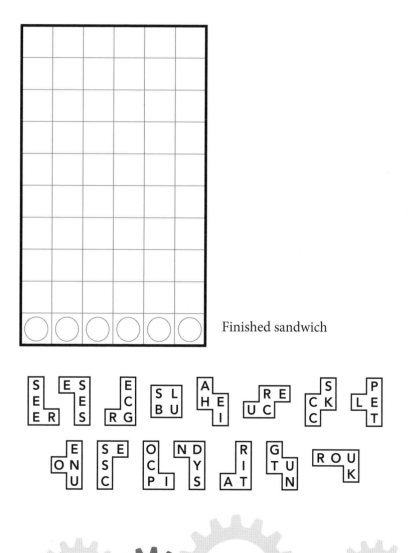

Finished sandwich

Numcross 18

Use the provided clues to fill the grid with numbers.
No entry may start with a 0.

A	B		C	D	E		F	G	H
I			J				K		
L		M				N			
		O		P	Q				
R	S			T			U	V	W
X				Y			Z		
			AA			BB			
CC	DD	EE				FF		GG	HH
II				JJ	KK			LL	
MM				NN				OO	

Across

A. A perfect square

C. A down – D down

F. Consecutive digits in ascending order

I. 2 × D down

J. B down in reverse

K. 2 × T across

L. An anagram of C down

N. GG down × I across

O. 12 × N across

R. CC down + 1

T. 5 × JJ down

U. GG down – 1

X. GG down – 5

Y. A perfect cube

Z. C across – N down

AA. Contains one of each odd digit

CC. 2 × G down

FF. B down × 12

II. Consecutive digits in ascending order

JJ. Another perfect square

LL. Another perfect square

MM. A palindrome

NN. G down + T across

OO. 2 × I across

Down

A. LL across × 4

B. J across in reverse

C. Z across × R down

D. R down - 1

E. Y across in reverse

F. X across × 4

G. Another palindrome

H. N down squared

M. One-fifth of AA across

N. D down + I across

P. The 'Summer of Love'

Q. Consecutive digits in descending order

R. D down + 1

S. Another perfect cube

U. 2 × MM across

V. R down × 8

W. Sum of the digits in the fifth column from left (D down, P down, and JJ down)

AA. Another perfect square

BB. M down in reverse

CC. I across + J across

DD. U across × 4

EE. H down + E down

GG. E down × 4

HH. N down × 7

JJ. KK down – N down

KK. Another perfect square

Black Holes 11

Divide the grid into chunks along the guides
provided so that each chunk contains one black
hole, and so the digits in the chunk sum to the
number in the black hole.

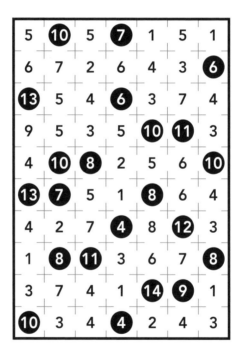

In Memoriam 4A

Memorize the images displayed below. When you're
ready, turn the page and put your memory to the test.

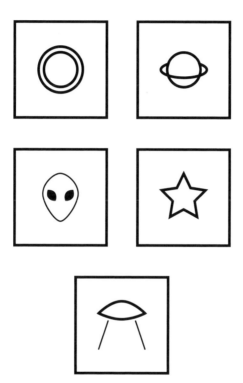

In Memoriam 4B

Moving up, down, left, and right, make a path from Start to Finish. You may only pass through squares containing an image displayed on the previous page.

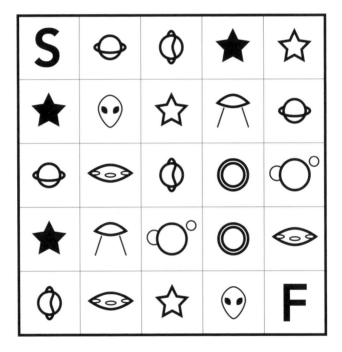

Chess Sudoku 6

Place a digit from 1 to 8 into each empty cell so that each row, column, and 3x3 block contains each digit once, without repetition. The chess knights in the grid display the sum of the digits in the cells which they can attack.

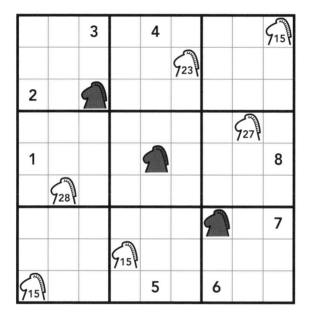

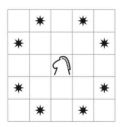

Tetra Grid 20

Drop each of the shapes into the grid in the order provided to spell ten six-letter words. Clues for the words have been provided next to the grid.

One in charge

Take away

Investments

Shower nuisance

Frugal person's clipping

Audible warnings

Type of card

Flowery quality

Potential sale location

Hot dog topper

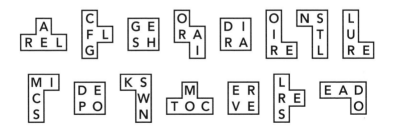

In Memoriam 5A

Memorize the numbers shown in the grid below.
When you're ready, turn the page and put your
memory to the test.

S	1	4	0	8
9	0	2	1	0
8	6	7	5	3
0	9	3	2	1
1	8	0	0	F

In Memoriam 5B

Moving up, down, left, and right, make a path from
Start to Finish. You may only pass through squares
where the number has not changed from the number
that was in the same square on the previous page.

S	1	4	0	8
7	1	1	9	0
8	6	7	5	3
4	0	4	2	6
1	8	8	0	F

Rearrangement 35–36

Rearrange the letters in the phrase "WORST ORACLE" to spell something useful for a painter pretending to be a psychic.

Rearrange the letters in the phrase "A TEST PHOTO" to spell a product often advertised with before and after photos.

Cube Logic 19

Which two of the six foldable patterns can be folded
to make the same cube?

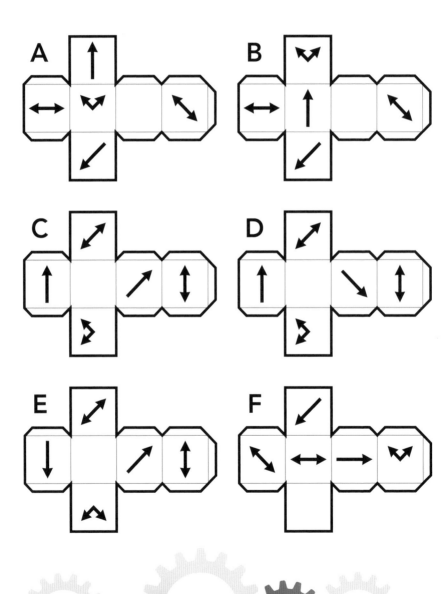

Rows Garden 8

Using the clues provided, enter a letter into each triangle to fill the garden. Each row contains one or two entries, and each hexagonal flower contains a six-letter word wrapped around the center. It's up to you to determine where to place the starting letter and the direction of the word.

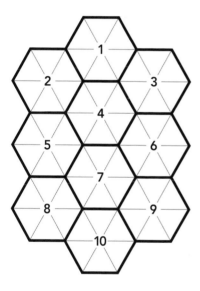

Primate

Inky sea-dweller/Judge

Rub out/Luxury hotel brand

Full range/Microsoft search engine

Disputed Asian region/Ugly giant

Oft-chaotic bird/Queue

Antagonists/"Double D" in toon trio

Common address suffix

Flowers

1. Made good on a loan
2. Simple shape
3. Convict
4. Absurd
5. Calculated risk

6. Spicy root
7. Mexican street corn
8. Legume nickname
9. Refused
10. Goes away

Tetra Grid 21A

Drop each of the shapes into the grid in the order provided to spell ten six-letter words. Clues for the words have been provided next to the grid.

X-Files agent

Root vegetable

Book creator

Ringed planet

Holey breakfast items

City in Minnesota

On the web?

Three-ringed noun

Secondary color

Health insurance add-on

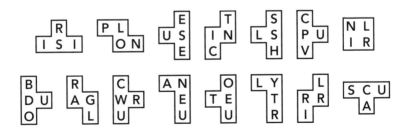

Tetra Grid 21B

Drop each of the shapes into the grid in the order
provided to spell ten NEW six-letter words which
match up with the clues from the previous puzzle.

X-Files agent

Root vegetable

Book creator

Ringed planet

Holey breakfast items

City in Minnesota

On the web?

Three-ringed noun

Secondary color

Health insurance add-on

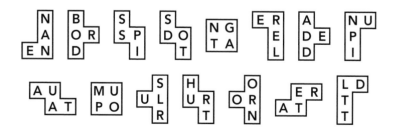

Numcross 19

Use the provided clues to fill the grid with numbers.
No entry may start with a 0.

A	B	C	D		E	F		G	H
I					J		K		
		L		M		N			
O	P		Q		R			S	T
U		V		W			X		
Y			Z				AA		
BB			CC			DD		EE	
		FF			GG		HH		
II	JJ			KK		LL		MM	NN
OO			PP			QQ			

Across

A. I across + 5000

E. E down – 1

G. One-fourth of S across

I. C down + 200

J. Consecutive digits in ascending order

L. B down × E across

N. NN down – 1

O. G across + 2

Q. Consecutive digits in descending order

S. EE across + 7

U. One-half of LL across

W. M down × KK down

Y. A palindrome

AA. EE across + MM down

BB. B down – 1

CC. An anagram of LL across

EE. LL across / S across

FF. A perfect cube

GG. KK down × X down

II. 2 × Z down

LL. Year that QQ across was released

OO. II down in reverse

PP. HH down – GG across

QQ. A Stanley Kubrick film

Down

A. G down in reverse

B. A down – K down

C. I across – 200

D. A down × B down × 5

E. B down × 3

F. C down × KK down

G. A perfect square

H. A perfect cube

K. MM down – BB across

M. Contains one of each even digit

O. LL across + 3

P. N across × MM down

R. Contains one of each odd digit

S. Another palindrome

T. Digits that sum to BB down

V. G down + KK down

X. KK down – 4

Z. One-half of II across

DD. G across × AA across

FF. FF across + 5

HH. GG across + PP across

II. Another perfect square

JJ. S across – KK down

KK. Another perfect square

MM. BB across × 6

NN. One more perfect square for good measure

Symbol Sums 22

The sums of five combinations of symbols have been
provided. What is the value of each individual symbol?

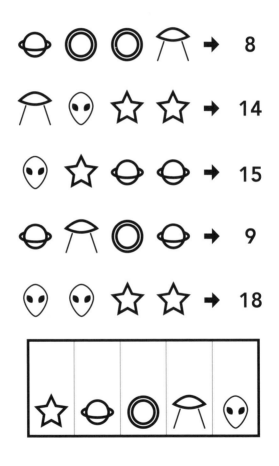

Rearrangement 37–38

Rearrange the letters in the phrase "INLAND PARLEY" to spell the place a pirate might write down a memo for such an event.

Rearrange the letters in the phrase "COOL TORMENTER" to spell something that could be used to interrupt a binge-watching session.

Black Holes 12

Divide the grid into chunks along the guides provided so that each chunk contains one black hole, and so the digits in the chunk sum to the number in the black hole.

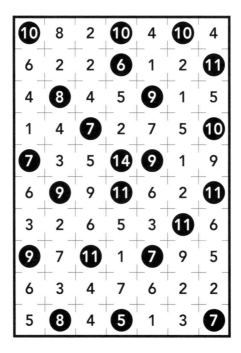

In Memoriam 6A

Memorize the numbers shown in the balls below.
When you're ready, turn the page and put your
memory to the test.

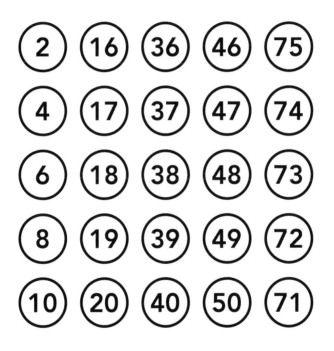

In Memoriam 6B

In the grid below, find the single row, column,
or diagonal that contains only numbers from the
previous page. (Yelling "BINGO" when you're done
is optional.)

2	29	32	56	75
6	17	39	46	72
8	28	Free Space	51	68
4	26	35	49	71
1	20	40	60	70

Tetra Grid 22

Drop each of the shapes into the grid in the order
provided to spell ten six-letter words. Clues for the
words have been provided next to the grid.

Sewing unit

Arrow holder

Type of mushroom

Leave

Smashing Pumpkins frontman

Pulse

Bed necessity

Heat

Workout component

Repaired

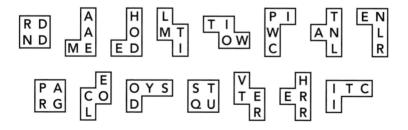

Cube Logic 20

Which two of the six foldable patterns can be folded
to make the same cube?

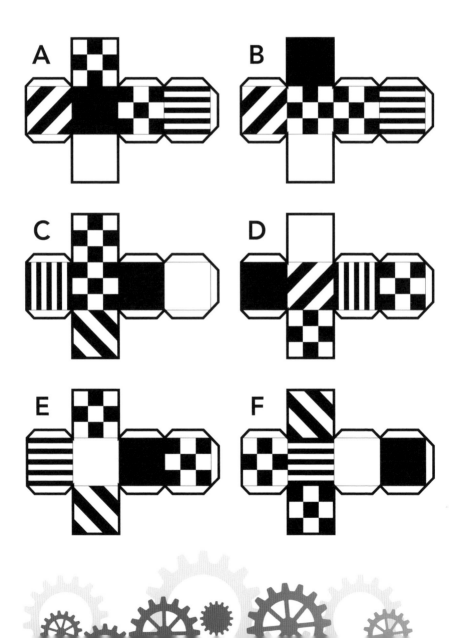

ANSWER KEYS

Arrow Maze 1

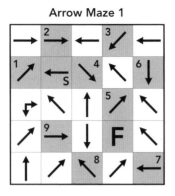

Arrow Maze 2

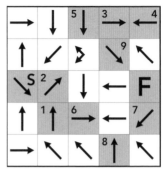

Arrow Maze 3

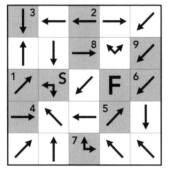

Arrow Maze 4

Arrow Maze 5

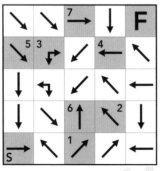

Arrow Maze 6

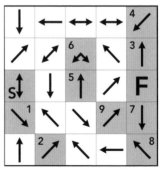

Arrow Maze 7

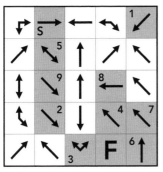

Arrow Maze 8

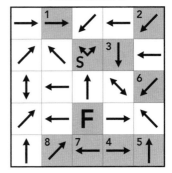

Arrow Maze 9

Arrow Maze 10

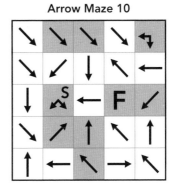

Black Holes 1

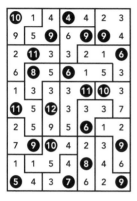

Black Holes 2

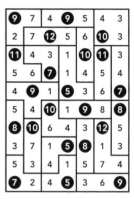

Black Holes 3

Black Holes 4

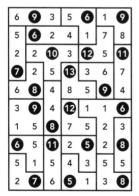

Black Holes 5

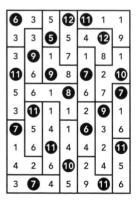

Black Holes 6

Black Holes 7

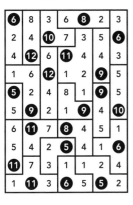

Black Holes 8

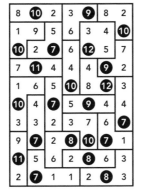

Black Holes 9

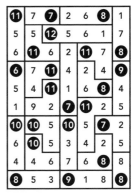

Black Holes 10

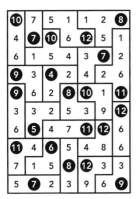

Black Holes 11

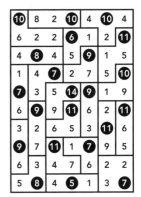

Black Holes 12

Chess Sudoku 1

4	5	2	7	3	6	8	♞	1
♞	1	6	8	2	4	5	3	7
8	7	3	1	5	♞	4	2	6
5	2	♞	3	8	7	1	6	4
6	4	7	2	♞	1	3	5	8
3	8	1	4	6	5	♞	7	2
7	3	8	♞	4	2	6	1	5
1	6	4	5	7	3	2	8	♞
2	♞	5	6	1	8	7	4	3

Chess Sudoku 2

1	7	8	6	4	♞	2	5	3
5	2	♞	3	7	1	8	6	4
4	6	3	5	2	8	1	♞	7
♞	5	7	4	8	2	3	1	6
3	1	2	7	♞	6	4	8	5
6	8	4	1	3	5	7	2	♞
7	♞	5	8	1	3	6	4	2
8	3	6	2	5	4	♞	7	1
2	4	1	♞	6	7	5	3	8

Chess Sudoku 3

7	6	1	3	4	8	♞	2	5
5	8	3	♞	7	2	1	6	4
♞	2	4	5	6	1	7	8	3
8	4	7	1	2	5	3	♞	5
2	1	5	6	♞	3	4	7	8
3	♞	6	4	8	7	2	5	1
6	7	2	8	1	4	5	3	♞
4	5	8	7	3	♞	6	1	2
1	3	♞	2	5	6	8	4	7

Chess Sudoku 4

5	7	1	6	4	8	♞	3	2
3	6	2	♞	1	7	5	4	8
♞	8	4	2	5	3	1	7	6
4	♞	7	3	8	2	6	5	1
6	1	8	4	♞	5	3	2	7
2	5	3	7	6	1	8	♞	4
7	2	5	8	3	6	4	1	♞
1	4	6	5	7	♞	2	8	3
8	3	♞	1	2	4	7	6	5

Chess Sudoku 5

2	8	♞	3	1	4	6	7	5
1	4	7	6	5	♞	8	2	3
3	6	5	2	7	8	4	1	♞
4	♞	2	1	8	5	3	6	7
5	1	3	7	♞	6	2	8	4
8	7	6	4	2	3	5	♞	1
♞	3	4	8	6	7	1	5	2
6	5	1	♞	4	2	7	3	8
7	2	8	5	3	1	♞	4	6

Chess Sudoku 6

8	5	3	6	4	7	2	1	♞
6	7	1	5	2	♞	8	3	4
2	4	♞	1	8	3	5	7	6
4	6	8	3	7	5	1	♞	2
1	3	5	2	♞	4	7	6	8
7	♞	2	8	1	6	3	4	5
5	8	6	4	3	1	♞	2	7
3	2	7	♞	6	8	4	5	1
♞	1	4	7	5	2	6	8	3

Cube Logic

1:	Pattern D	6:	Pattern A	11:	Pattern D	16:	Pattern D
2:	Pattern C	7:	Pattern B	12:	Pattern A	17:	Pattern B
3:	Pattern B	8:	Pattern A	13:	Pattern C	18:	Patterns B and F
4:	Pattern D	9:	Pattern C	14:	Pattern B	19:	Patterns A and C
5:	Pattern A	10:	Pattern D	15:	Pattern A	20:	Patterns D and F

In Memoriam 1

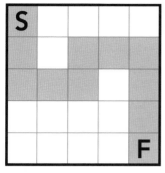

In Memoriam 2

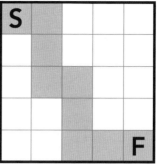

In Memoriam 3

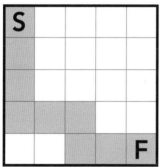

In Memoriam 4

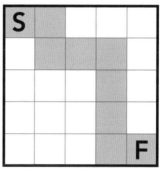

In Memoriam 5

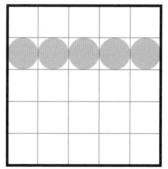

In Memoriam 6

Maze 1

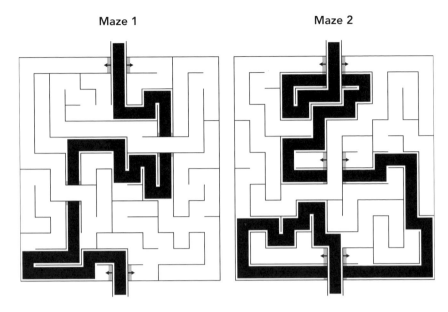

Maze 2

Maze 3

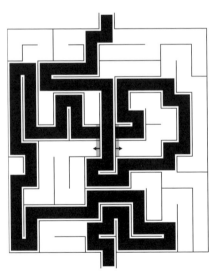

Maze 4

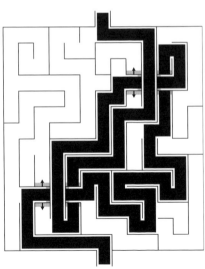

Numcross 1
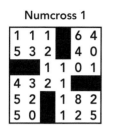

Numcross 2

Numcross 3

Numcross 4
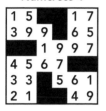

Numcross 5

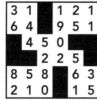

Numcross 6

Numcross 7
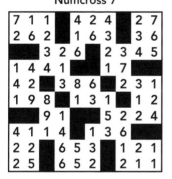

Numcross 8

(continued)

Numcross 9

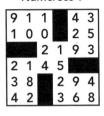

Numcross 10

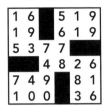

Numcross 11

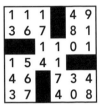

Numcross 12

Numcross 13

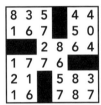

Numcross 14

Numcross 15

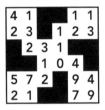

Numcross 16

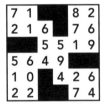

Numcross 17

Numcross 18

Numcross 19

Pent Words 1

C	R	A	F	T
T	O	W	E	R
A	N	V	I	L
P	L	A	T	E
E	R	A	S	E

Pent Words 2

P	A	I	N	T
S	T	E	A	L
S	A	L	O	N
L	E	V	E	E
O	P	E	N	S

Pent Words 3

B	L	E	N	D
A	M	I	G	O
B	E	L	O	W
R	I	G	O	R
S	I	G	H	T

Pent Words 4

L	E	M	O	N
C	U	R	S	E
R	E	A	C	T
S	M	O	K	E
T	E	A	M	S

Pent Words 5

S	P	A	D	E
T	R	I	A	L
R	I	D	G	E
P	R	E	E	N
I	N	S	E	T

Pent Words 6

S	T	E	E	L
S	P	R	I	G
M	O	U	T	H
A	P	A	R	T
Z	E	S	T	Y

Pent Words 7

S	H	A	P	E
R	A	C	E	R
P	L	E	A	D
P	E	A	R	L
R	I	G	H	T

Pent Words 8

B	I	S	O	N
P	O	L	A	R
A	M	O	N	G
R	E	E	L	S
S	E	V	E	N

Rearrangement

1: Flying Saucer
2: Carrot Cake
3: Highway Traffic
4: Tornado Alley
5: Pacific Coast Highway
6: Chili Cheese Fries
7: Talk Radio
8: Water Slide
9: Sparkling Water
10: Cast Iron Skillet
11: Honey Butter
12: Rest Areas
13: Virus Scanner
14: Monkey Bars
15: Vineyards
16: Chicken Soup
17: Hard Lemonade
18: Spare Tire

(continued)

Rearrangement

19:	Coffee Filters
20:	Batman and Robin
21:	Railroad Crossing
22:	Thirty Yard Line
23:	Roller Coasters
24:	Texas Panhandle
25:	Ariana Grande
26:	Chinese Takeout
27:	Binge Watching
28:	Income Taxes
29:	Radio Station
30:	Cell Signal
31:	Cast-Iron Pan
32:	Commuter Train
33:	Space Shuttle
34:	Fitted Sheets
35:	Watercolors
36:	Toothpaste
37:	Daily Planner
38:	Remote Control

Ringed Planet 1

E D
E K P E
D C I T
D E R A
S L C B
E A Y B
S S

Ringed Planet 2

E D
E R D V
P S A E
I N T N
S R U O
I A C S
T E

Ringed Planet 3

S T
N I O M
R P L S
U T A R
C E N G
T S T S
Y R

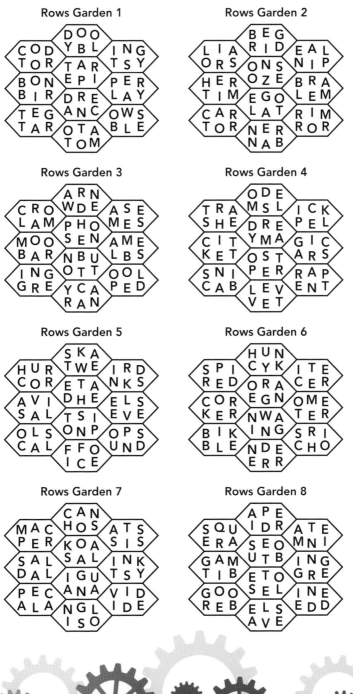

Rows Garden 1

Rows Garden 2

Rows Garden 3

Rows Garden 4

Rows Garden 5

Rows Garden 6

Rows Garden 7

Rows Garden 8

Story Logic 1
3:30 PM: Toyota, Supreme wash, Berried Treasure scent.
4:00 PM: Jeep, Express wash, Brisk Lake scent.
4:30 PM: Honda, Plus wash, Hot Breeze scent.
5:00 PM: Ford, Basic wash, Tropical Wood scent.

Story Logic 2
Fourth Place: Tanya's lentil-based Tikka Masala burger.
Third Place: Rakesh's mushroom-based Au Jus-Style burger.
Second Place: Sal's black bean-based Teriyaki burger.
First Place: Victor's tempeh-based Southwest burger.

Story Logic 3
Ms. Campbell on Ninth St.: Refrigerator in container DM446
Mr. Daivari on Owosso St.: Dryer in container AB456
Mr. Evans on Palm Ridge Way: Washer in container CC341
Mrs. Fredrickson on Mulberry St.: Stove in container CC179

Story Logic 4
Frankie: black with orange eyes, flaked tuna, neck scratches.
Nina Bean: small and gray, diced chicken, back rubs.
Ruby: black with green eyes, beef chunks, chin scratches.
Sailor: large and gray, beef pâté, head scratches.

Story Logic 5
Pacific Time: Red branding, 57 locations, run by Nanette.
Mountain Time: Blue branding, 59 locations, run by Kelsey.
Central Time: Purple branding, 47 locations, run by Myka.
Eastern Time: Green branding, 33 locations, run by Lance.

Story Logic 6
Country: Lindsay beat Lana and Vick
Hip-Hop: Mac beat Mark and Uma
Pop: Jai beat Nate and Tess
Rock: Keisha beat Kirk and Sasha

Story Logic 7   Kayla, the mechanic, lives 45 min. away and brought cookies.
Lenore, the cashier, lives 20 min. away and brought a hot dish.
Michael, the doctor, lives 57 min. away and brought a Jello mold.
Ned, the firefighter, lives 32 min. away and brought pasta salad.

Story Logic 8   Section 1: a cavern, with Mekala dressed as a skeleton
Section 2: a crypt, with Kiera dressed as a vampire
Section 3: a jail, with Jared dressed as a zombie
Section 4: a cemetery, with Nupur dressed as a goblin
Section 5: a sawmill, with Landon dressed as a mummy

Story Logic 9   Sunday's class at Georgie's is a sugar skull painting
Monday's class at The Brewery is a winter scene painting
Tuesday's class at Tres Amigas is a painting of mountains
Wednesday's class at The Tin Panther is a sunset painting

Story Logic 10   At 2.5 mi., a 60 ft. bridge dedicated to Becky Lynch
At 2.7 mi., a 20 ft. bridge dedicated to Leah Remini
At 8.1 mi., a 40 ft. bridge dedicated to Guy Fieri
At 8.3 mi., a 32 ft. bridge dedicated to Adam Savage
At 9.0 mi., a 48 ft. bridge dedicated to David Biedny

Story Logic 11   In 5th place, Amy's Cheezy Cauliflower Queso Dip
In 4th place, Carol's Smoked Almond Cheeze Ball
In 3rd place, Dirk's Nooch-oh Cheeze Sauce
In 2nd place, Eileen's Carrot Cheddar Chunks
In 1st place, Breighdynn's Wild Garlic Walnut Gouda Spread

Symbol Sums 1

15	8	11	7	6

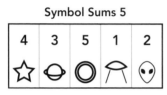

Symbol Sums 2

7	10	2	19	11

Symbol Sums 3

29	6	11	8	7

Symbol Sums 4

1	5	3	9	16

Symbol Sums 5

4	3	5	1	2

Symbol Sums 6

32	5	14	11	9

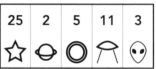

Symbol Sums 7

10	8	7	6	9

Symbol Sums 8

25	2	5	11	3

Symbol Sums 9

5	12	13	10	7

Symbol Sums 10

5	25	4	7	10

Symbol Sums 11

6	8	12	14	16

Symbol Sums 12

7	12	11	8	19

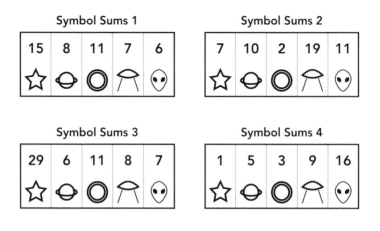

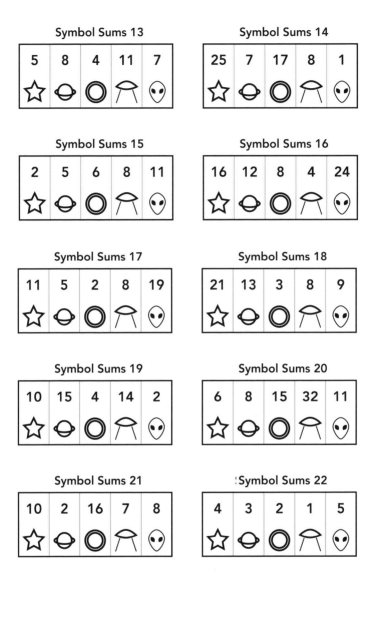

Symbol Sums 13

5	8	4	11	7

Symbol Sums 14

25	7	17	8	1

Symbol Sums 15

2	5	6	8	11

Symbol Sums 16

16	12	8	4	24

Symbol Sums 17

11	5	2	8	19

Symbol Sums 18

21	13	3	8	9

Symbol Sums 19

10	15	4	14	2

Symbol Sums 20

6	8	15	32	11

Symbol Sums 21

10	2	16	7	8

Symbol Sums 22

4	3	2	1	5

Tetra Grid 1

A	L	M	O	N	D
D	E	P	A	R	T
S	E	A	S	O	N
B	R	U	N	C	H
M	O	M	E	N	T
N	U	M	B	E	R
R	I	B	B	O	N
C	A	M	E	R	A
M	A	S	T	E	R
G	L	U	T	E	N

Tetra Grid 2

P	A	N	D	E	R
B	L	O	N	D	E
A	L	A	S	K	A
O	R	A	N	G	E
B	A	S	K	E	T
S	P	R	O	U	T
C	O	F	F	E	E
B	A	K	E	R	Y
S	T	R	O	N	G
F	R	A	N	C	E

Tetra Grid 3

H	A	W	A	I	I
G	A	R	D	E	N
B	U	R	G	E	R
S	K	E	T	C	H
T	A	C	K	L	E
V	I	S	I	O	N
B	O	U	N	C	E
G	E	R	M	A	N
H	E	A	L	T	H
B	E	A	N	I	E

Tetra Grid 4

C	O	M	E	D	Y
M	I	N	I	O	N
P	A	R	I	S	H
M	A	R	B	L	E
T	H	R	I	F	T
C	H	E	R	R	Y
T	H	R	O	N	E
P	I	R	A	T	E
S	T	R	I	P	E
F	E	L	O	N	Y

Tetra Grid 5

E	N	E	R	G	Y
O	U	T	A	G	E
D	E	L	U	G	E
M	O	R	B	I	D
F	O	R	G	E	T
P	U	R	P	L	E
S	C	R	A	P	E
C	A	R	P	E	T
T	H	R	I	L	L
F	L	O	W	E	R

Tetra Grid 6

B	A	T	T	L	E
S	N	E	E	Z	E
R	E	L	I	S	H
F	I	E	S	T	A
B	Y	P	A	S	S
M	I	N	C	E	D
C	H	E	E	R	Y
S	T	U	R	D	Y
A	M	U	S	E	D
D	E	F	I	N	E

Tetra Grid 7

P	O	R	T	A	L
F	O	R	E	S	T
D	I	L	U	T	E
B	U	C	K	E	T
C	A	C	T	U	S
P	O	P	P	E	D
B	O	I	L	E	R
D	E	N	T	A	L
R	E	B	A	T	E
I	R	O	N	E	D

Tetra Grid 8

R	E	L	O	A	D
C	R	E	A	T	E
S	P	R	I	N	G
D	R	E	N	C	H
T	A	B	L	E	T
D	I	A	B	L	O
P	R	O	V	E	N
R	I	B	B	O	N
D	R	E	N	C	H
R	O	D	E	N	T

Tetra Grid 9

W	A	T	E	R	Y
S	C	R	O	L	L
H	O	O	D	I	E
D	E	P	L	O	Y
D	E	S	I	G	N
C	A	T	T	L	E
T	Y	P	I	S	T
M	E	L	T	E	D
S	P	I	R	A	L
D	R	A	W	E	R

Tetra Grid 10

```
C O P P E R
C H A T T Y
F R I D G E
S E L D O M
C I T R U S
F I L T E R
P O C K E T
S T R E E T
E N I G M A
M O N D A Y
```

Tetra Grid 11

```
A N I M A L
T O M A T O
P E A N U T
L U M B E R
B A T T L E
F I E S T A
H E A R T S
E L E V E N
B R I G H T
S C R U B S
```

Tetra Grid 12

```
S P R I N G
W A S H E R
T R I V I A
K E R N E L
S P R O U T
B R U N C H
F R I G I D
D E X T E R
P O L A N D
G R A I N Y
```

Tetra Grid 13

```
F A U C E T
K I D N E Y
S M O O T H
C I R C L E
H O L L O W
B U T T E R
S I M P L E
D A N I S H
T R A V E L
S T A M P S
```

Tetra Grid 14

```
L E A V E S
S H R I M P
M A S C O T
D R I V E N
L I Q U O R
T A T T O O
M A T U R E
V E N D O R
B R I D G E
G R A V E L
```

Tetra Grid 15

```
E R A S E R
R E T U R N
L I C H E N
O R E G O N
W A F F L E
M E T E R S
R E V I V E
D E C A D E
C A N D L E
T R A G I C
```

Tetra Grid 16

```
E N E R G Y
A L M O S T
S P I C E D
L I Q U I D
A S S U M E
U R G E N T
S M O K E R
M I N I O N
B A R B E R
U N R E A D
```

Tetra Grid 17

```
D R I V E R
Y A N K E E
C O U G A R
S I Z Z L E
M A R K E R
S E N A T E
A M B U S H
C A M E R A
V O W E L S
P O L I C Y
```

Tetra Grid 18

```
S C R I P T
C O U R S E
R A P T O R
S I S T E R
L O C K E T
S T R E A M
R E W A R D
V I O L E T
M E D I U M
B U B B L E
```

(continued)

Tetra Grid 19A

G	R	O	U	N	D
S	E	S	A	M	E
T	A	H	I	N	I
F	R	O	Z	E	N
Y	O	G	U	R	T
C	H	E	R	R	Y
P	E	A	N	U	T
P	I	E	C	E	S
B	A	N	A	N	A
S	P	L	I	T	S

Tetra Grid 19B

G	R	O	U	N	D
T	U	R	K	E	Y
O	N	I	O	N	S
C	A	T	S	U	P
P	I	C	K	L	E
S	E	C	R	E	T
S	A	U	C	E	S
C	H	E	E	S	E
S	L	I	C	E	S
B	U	R	G	E	R

Tetra Grid 20

L	E	A	D	E	R
R	E	M	O	V	E
S	T	O	C	K	S
M	I	L	D	E	W
C	O	U	P	O	N
S	I	R	E	N	S
C	R	E	D	I	T
F	L	O	R	A	L
G	A	R	A	G	E
R	E	L	I	S	H

Tetra Grid 21A

S	C	U	L	L	Y
C	A	R	R	O	T
W	R	I	T	E	R
U	R	A	N	U	S
B	A	G	E	L	S
D	U	L	U	T	H
O	N	L	I	N	E
C	I	R	C	U	S
P	U	R	P	L	E
V	I	S	I	O	N

Tetra Grid 21B

M	U	L	D	E	R
P	O	T	A	T	O
A	U	T	H	O	R
S	A	T	U	R	N
D	O	N	U	T	S
S	T	P	A	U	L
S	P	I	D	E	R
B	I	N	D	E	R
O	R	A	N	G	E
D	E	N	T	A	L

Tetra Grid 22

S	T	I	T	C	H
Q	U	I	V	E	R
O	Y	S	T	E	R
D	E	P	A	R	T
C	O	R	G	A	N
L	E	N	T	I	L
P	I	L	L	O	W
W	A	R	M	T	H
C	A	R	D	I	O
M	E	N	D	E	D

UFO Sighting

1: Flour, Tofurky, Founder, Outfit, Fortune

2: Soulful, Fourth, Focus, Furor, Futon

Word Sudoku 1

N	T	P	O	S	H
O	S	H	N	T	P
P	N	S	H	O	T
H	O	T	P	N	S
S	P	O	T	H	N
T	H	N	S	P	O

Word Sudoku 2

T	O	B	S	R	I
I	S	R	O	B	T
O	R	T	B	I	S
S	B	I	R	T	O
B	I	S	T	O	R
R	T	O	I	S	B

Word Sudoku 3

Y	U	M	E	R	C
M	C	R	Y	E	U
C	E	Y	U	M	R
R	M	E	C	U	Y
E	Y	U	R	C	M
U	R	C	M	Y	E

Word Sudoku 4

L	T	E	P	N	A
E	P	N	A	L	T
N	L	A	T	P	E
P	A	T	N	E	L
A	E	P	L	T	N
T	N	L	E	A	P

Word Sudoku 5

S	U	R	A	N	T
T	A	N	R	U	S
U	R	T	N	S	A
A	N	S	U	T	R
N	S	A	T	R	U
R	T	U	S	A	N

Word Sudoku 6

A	L	O	M	N	P
M	P	N	L	A	O
O	A	P	N	L	M
L	N	M	O	P	A
N	M	A	P	O	L
P	O	L	A	M	N

Word Sudoku 7

T	R	E	O	K	C
K	C	O	R	E	T
E	K	C	T	R	O
R	O	T	K	C	E
C	T	K	E	O	R
O	E	R	C	T	K

Word Sudoku 8

E	N	T	C	I	S
S	C	I	E	N	T
T	I	E	S	C	N
C	S	N	T	E	I
N	T	C	I	S	E
I	E	S	N	T	C

Word Sudoku 9

S	L	E	C	P	I
P	S	C	I	E	L
E	C	P	L	I	S
C	I	L	P	S	E
L	E	I	S	C	P
I	P	S	E	L	C

Thanks for solving!

Exercise Your Mind at American Mensa

At American Mensa, we love puzzles. In fact, we have events—large and small—centered around games and puzzles.

Of course, with tens of thousands of members from ages 2 to 102, we are much more than that. Our one shared trait might be one you share, too: high intelligence, measured in the top 2 percent of the general public in a standardized test.

Get-togethers with other Mensans—from small pizza nights up to larger events like our annual Mind Games®—are always stimulating and fun. Roughly 130 Special Interest Groups (we call them SIGs) offer the best of the real and virtual worlds. Highlighting the Mensa newsstand is our award-winning magazine, *Mensa Bulletin*, which stimulates the curious mind with unique features that add perspective to our fast-paced world.

And then there are the practical benefits of membership, such as exclusive offers through our partners and member discounts on magazine subscriptions, online shopping, and financial services.

Find out how to qualify or take our practice test at americanmensa.org/join.